THE EPISTLES OF JOHN

THE EPISTLES
OF JOHN

Introduction, Exposition and Notes

BY

F. F. BRUCE

WILLIAM B. EERDMANS PUBLISHING COMPANY
GRAND RAPIDS, MICHIGAN

First published 1970 by Pickering & Inglis Ltd. This
American edition published 1979 through special ar-
rangement with Pickering & Inglis by Wm. B. Eerdmans
Publishing Company, Grand Rapids, Michigan.

Reprinted, February 1992

Library of Congress Cataloging in Publication Data

Bruce, Frederick Fyvie, 1910-
    The Epistles of John

    "The Bible text . . . is the Revised version of 1881."
    "The substance of this commentary appeared in
twenty-four installments in the Witness during 1967
and 1968."
    Bibliography: p. 20.
    Includes index.
    1. Bible. N.T. Epistles of John — Commentaries.
I. Bible. N.T. Epistles of John. English. Revised. 1979.
II. Title.
BS2805.3.B77 1979   227'.94'077   78-22069
ISBN 0-8028-1783-1

TO

PAT AND PAMELA

PREFACE

THE substance of this commentary appeared in twenty-four instalments in *The Witness* during 1967 and 1968. It is mainly due to the friendly insistence of the Editor of *The Witness*, Mr. G. C. D. Howley, that the work was undertaken in the first instance.

Like my exposition of Ephesians, published in 1961, these studies are intended chiefly for the general Christian reader who is interested in serious Bible study, not for the professional or specialist student. Textual, linguistic and other critical questions have been touched on lightly; the main aim has been to bring out the meaning and message of the three Epistles. The professional student may, however, find some help in a number of the notes which have been added for the publication of the work in book form, especially in those which provide bibliographical information on matters of exegetical importance.

The Bible text on which the exposition is based is the Revised Version of 1881, since that is the most literal of all the standard renderings of the Greek text. Other versions, however, have been freely utilized.

August, 1970   F.F.B.

CONTENTS

ABBREVIATIONS

AV	Authorized (King James) Version
BJRL	*Bulletin of the John Rylands Library* (Manchester)
CSEL	*Corpus Scriptorum Ecclesiasticorum Latinorum*
Hist. Eccl.	*Ecclesiastical History* (Eusebius)
JBL	*Journal of Biblical Literature*
JTS	*Journal of Theological Studies*
LXX	Septuagint (Greek Old Testament)
NEB	New English Bible
NT	New Testament
NTS	*New Testament Studies*
OT	Old Testament
RSV	Revised Standard Version
RV	Revised Version
TDNT	*Theological Dictionary of the New Testament*, edited by G. Kittel and G. Friedrich, English translation by G. W. Bromiley (Eerdmans, Grand Rapids, 1964–)
TEV	Today's English Version (Good News for Modern Man)
TU	*Texte und Untersuchungen*
ZTK	*Zeitschrift für Theologie und Kirche*

GENERAL INTRODUCTION

I BACKGROUND AND OCCASION OF THE THREE EPISTLES

The Roman province of Asia occupied roughly the western third of the peninsula which we call Asia Minor. The Romans gave it the name of Asia because it was the first territory on the continent of Asia to come under the direct control of the Roman state. For a century and a half before its incorporation in the Roman Empire, this territory had constituted the kingdom of Pergamum, whose rulers were friends and allies of Rome. When the last king of Pergamum died, in 133 BC, he bequeathed his realm to the Roman senate and people, and after deliberation they decided to accept the bequest. After reorganization as a Roman province, it was governed by a senior ex-magistrate called a proconsul, who was appointed by the senate, normally for one year. The province is therefore referred to sometimes as 'proconsular Asia'. To begin with, the proconsul's seat of government was at Pergamum, the capital of the former kingdom, but later it was moved to Ephesus, and there it remained throughout New Testament times. Asia was regarded as the wealthiest of the Roman provinces; its cities had been centres of Greek culture for many centuries.

Christianity may have been introduced to the province of Asia by individuals before the middle of the first century AD, but it was effectively established in the province during Paul's Ephesian ministry, to be dated probably from the late summer of AD 52 to the spring of 55. So thoroughly did Paul and his colleagues prosecute the work of evangelization during those years that not only the people of Ephesus but 'all the residents of Asia heard the word of the Lord, both Jews and Greeks' (Acts 19. 10). The seven churches of Revelation, and other churches besides, were founded at that time, and the continuous history of Christianity in that territory can be traced from then until the Graeco-Turkish exchange of populations in 1923.

The intellectual activity of the cities of Asia could not leave the gospel unaffected. Among the Jews of the province – especially in Asian Phrygia, its most easterly region – there is ample contemporary evidence of syncretism in life and thought, of the fusion of their ancestral beliefs and practices with features from the older ethnic religions of Asia Minor and from more recent mystery cults and philosophical trends. The same sort of thing was not long in making its appearance among the Christians of the province. There is an ominous note in Paul's Miletus address to the elders of the Ephesian church, when they are warned that from their own ranks 'will arise men speaking perverse things, to draw away the disciples after them' (Acts 20. 30). An outstanding example of the threat presented by syncretistic tendencies to the unique essence of Christianity is the 'Colossian heresy' which, only a few years after Paul's Ephesian ministry, was rife in the church of Colossae and other cities of the Lycus valley (in Asian Phrygia) and which is refuted in the Epistle to the Colossians (c. AD 61). Worse was to follow: a landslide away from apostolic teaching[1] is implied in the words of 2 Tim. 1. 15, 'You are aware that all who are in Asia turned away from me'.

The sixties of the first century, however, saw a welcome re-vitalizing of apostolic Christianity in proconsular Asia. This was due to the immigration of a number of Christians from Palestine shortly before the outbreak of the Jewish War in AD 66. These were not the more Judaistic members of the Jerusalem church who around the same time migrated to Transjordan, but outward-looking members of the church of Caesarea and other churches in the tradition of those Hellenistic believers who were dispersed after the martyrdom of Stephen and inaugurated the Gentile mission in Syrian Antioch and elsewhere. Those who migrated to pro-consular Asia included some very eminent Christians – Philip the evangelist and his daughters, for example, whose tombs were pointed out some generations later in Hierapolis in Asian Phrygia, and 'John the disciple of the Lord', who is associated mainly with Ephesus.[2] The identity of this John has been much discussed. Those writers who mention him regard him as a companion of our

Lord and an eyewitness of His ministry. More important for our purpose is his relation to the unnamed author of the three Epistles of John; suffice it to say that here it is accepted that the Epistles were written by this 'John the disciple of the Lord', and also that he is the Fourth Evangelist.[3]

John lived to a great age, until the time came when he was the sole survivor of those who had been in close contact with Jesus before His death and resurrection. It needs little imagination to understand how eagerly he would be sought out and listened to by people who valued first-hand information about the deeds and words of his Master and theirs. We know of two leaders in the Asian churches in the first half of the second century who never forgot what they had heard from John – Polycarp, bishop of Smyrna, who told his own young disciples in turn 'of his intercourse with John and the others who had seen the Lord',[4] and Papias, bishop of Hierapolis, who thought that what he could get from books would not help him so much as what came from 'a living and abiding voice'.[5]

These men, and others before them, attached special importance to the testimony of a man like John when teachers came along presenting a new brand of doctrine with the claim that it was the original and authentic doctrine of Christ – perhaps secretly committed by Him to chosen vessels and transmitted orally by them until the time was ripe for wider publicity. What were Christians to do or say when claims like these were put before them? A decision on their validity was not so easy to reach in days before the New Testament documents were collected and in general circulation. It was not altogether satisfactory to reply, 'This is quite different from what we have always been taught' – such a reply might betoken an excessively conservative clinging to tradition, and the new teachers might say that the doctrine which they brought was part of 'all the truth' into which Jesus said the Holy Spirit would lead His followers. Moreover, the new brand of doctrine would probably be so completely in accordance with the prevailing climate of opinion that in the eyes of many thinking people this was manifestly the way in which the gospel was to be 're-stated' for their day if it was to have any chance of acceptance and indeed survival.

One form of 're-stating' the gospel which was very much in keeping with the current climate of opinion at the end of the first Christian century was that which its critics called 'Docetism'.[6] It sprang from a dualistic interpretation of the world, widely accepted in those days, which viewed matter as essentially evil and spirit as essentially good. There could be no peaceful co-existence between the two; in particular, it was unthinkable that there could be any direct relation between the supreme God, who was pure spirit and essentially good, and the material universe, which by definition was essentially evil. The biblical doctrine of creation must therefore be jettisoned; the material universe must be regarded as the work of some inferior power or 'demiurge'.[7] The biblical doctrine of resurrection must also be jettisoned; it was unacceptable to the Greek mind in any case, as reactions to Paul's teaching in Athens and Corinth showed (Acts 17. 32; 1 Cor. 15. 12 ff.), but it was logically excluded by the dualistic world-view, which thought of the climax of redemption as the final liberation of the soul from its bodily shackles, not the receiving of a new (albeit 'spiritual') body as its vehicle of communication with a new environment.

It is in special relation to the person of Christ that this dualistic outlook gave rise to Docetism. The first disciples of Christ knew their Master to be a real human being; they also confessed him to be the Son of God, their Divine Lord. When this confession was understood, as it was by many Greek Christians, in metaphysical terms, it raised problems which were hotly debated in the great Christological controversies of the following centuries. To thorough-going dualists the problem was simply this: How could the true God indwell a human body of flesh and blood? The general Docetic answer to this problem was that, since such an indwelling was plainly impossible, the human body of flesh and blood was not a real one but an imaginary one; it only *seemed* to be so.[8] One special variety of Docetism is associated with the name of Cerinthus, who flourished in the nineties of the first century, and who is traditionally represented as the *bête noire* of John the disciple of the Lord.[9] Cerinthus, a man trained in Egypt but resident in the province of Asia, accepted the general dualistic world-view (including the creation of matter by an inferior power), but propounded a novel Christology. He distinguished the man Jesus (the son of Joseph and Mary, endowed with greater virtue and wisdom than other men), from 'the Christ', who descended on Jesus in the form of a dove after He was baptized, empowering Him to perform miracles and proclaim 'the unknown Father', but who left Him before He died, so that 'Jesus suffered and rose again, while the Christ remained immune from suffering, since He was a spiritual being'.[10] In spite of second-century tradition, however, it is not certain that it is his views exclusively that are controverted in 1 and 2 John.[11]

John writes with conscious authority, whether he is refuting the claims of those whose teaching denies that 'Jesus Christ has come in the flesh' or directing churches to welcome visitors who bring the true gospel but to give no countenance to any doctrine which is inconsistent with it. If in some places there is a tendency to disregard his authority, as there was in the church ruled by Diotrephes, he is confident that a personal visit will suffice to re-establish his authority; Diotrephes will be cut down to size. John's authority in this circle of churches is comparable to Paul's in his Gentile mission-field: 'I will come to you soon, if the Lord wills', writes Paul to the Corinthians, 'and I will find out not the talk of these arrogant people but their power' (1 Cor. 4. 19). But whereas Paul invokes the *apostolic* authority committed to him by the Lord, John does not argue in these terms; the word 'apostle' is absent from his Epistles, and in the Gospel it occurs only once, and that in the general sense of 'messenger' (John 13. 16, 'he who is sent'). John is the bearer and representative of what we should call 'apostolic tradition' (although he does not describe it as 'apostolic'); indeed, because of his personal association with the earliest days of Christianity, he is the embodiment of that tradition[12] – more particularly, the tradition as it is set forth in his Gospel.[13] This tradition, together with him who embodies it, is vested with the authority of the Lord Himself – not only because it stems from

Him as a matter of history but also because it is continuously validated by Him as the exalted and ever-living One, who is still active in the world by His Spirit in His servants.[14] This is the authority by which John acts and writes, and of those who repudiated his authority he might well say, like Paul, 'if I come again I will not spare them – since you desire proof that Christ is speaking in me' (2 Cor. 13. 2 f.).

II   THE THREE EPISTLES IN THE EARLY CHURCH

The first epistle of John was known in the province of Asia quite early in the second century. Ignatius, bishop of Antioch (martyred *c.* AD 110), has one or two *possible* allusions to it, especially in a passage in his letter to the Ephesian church where he speaks of the incarnation as 'God having become in flesh',[15] which could be a typically Ignatian paraphrase of 1 John 4. 2, 3. A telescoped quotation of these same two verses appears in Polycarp's letter to the Philippian church (*c.* AD 120),[16] and Polycarp's contemporary Papias is said by Eusebius to have 'made use of testimonies from the former epistle of John'.[17] Other second-century writers in whom traces of this epistle have been recognized are the Gnostic Valentinus,[18] Justin Martyr in Rome,[19] and the anonymous author of the *Letter to Diognetus*.[20]

Later in the century Irenaeus of Lyons[21] and Tertullian of Carthage[22] quote it explicitly and repeatedly, ascribing it to John the apostle and according it therefore unquestioned authority.

Towards the end of the second century two, if not three, of the epistles were not only known in the Roman church but recognized as canonical. The Muratorian list of New Testament books, drawn up at Rome *c.* AD 190 and preserved in a single incomplete Latin manuscript of the seventh or eighth century, discovered and published in 1740 by Cardinal L. A. Muratori (whence its designation) and now in the Ambrosian Library at Milan, gives a free quotation from the opening words of 1 John in connection with its account of the Fourth Gospel. The author of the list, wishing to emphasize that this Gospel presents the evidence of an eyewitness, goes on to say:

What wonder, then, that John in his epistles also should lay such bold claim to the following experiences, one by one, saying of himself: 'What we have seen with our eyes and heard with our ears and our hands have handled, this is what we write to you.' For in these words he claims to be not only a spectator and hearer, but also a writer of all the Lord's wonderful works in order.[23]

Later in the list two epistles 'of the aforementioned John' are said to be included *in catholica*,[24] which presumably means that they were accepted in the Catholic Church. The identity of these two is uncertain. The compiler of the list may mean two in addition to the one already quoted (i.e. 2 and 3 John in addition to 1 John);[25] he may mean 1 John together with one of the others or, if 2 and 3 John were taken together as one (which is not very probable), he may mean 1 John together with 2 and 3 John. Most probably he means 1 and 2 John. There is evidence that 3 John was rendered into Latin by another (and later?) translator than 1 and 2 John;[26] this being so, the Muratorian author, and the church whose New Testament canon he recorded, may well have known only 1 and 2 John. This was the situation at the same time in Alexandria: Clement of Alexandria appears to have known 1 and 2 John only,[27] whereas one or two generations later, in that same city, Origen and Dionysius knew 3 John as well. An African list of New Testament books of *c.* AD 360 (the Cheltenham or Mommsenian Canon) indicates that when it was drawn up 'three epistles of John' were recognized in the church of Carthage, but the added words 'one only' suggest that some conservative spirits were none too sure about 2 and 3 John. The evidence points to the canonical recognition of 1, 2 and 3 John in stages, one at a time.

Origen (*c.* AD 231) says that John 'has left an epistle of a very few lines and, it may be, a second and a third, for not all say that these [i.e. the second and the third] are genuine'.[28] According to Eusebius, writing *c.* AD 325, 1 John in his days belonged to the 'acknowledged books' (*homologoumena*), while 2 and 3 John were 'disputed' (*antilegomena*), because 'they might be the work of the evangelist or of someone else with the same name'.[29] The authorized version of the Bible in Syriac (the Peshitta), published early in the fifth century, included 1 John but not 2 and 3 John. Not until the Philoxenian version of AD 508 were these two epistles (with 2 Peter, Jude and Revelation) included in an edition of the Syriac New Testament.

The first epistle belongs properly to the group of New Testament documents called Catholic (or General) Epistles, because they are not addressed to any one person or community. Origen applies the epithet 'catholic' to 1 John;[30] his disciple Dionysius, bishop of Alexandria, also speaks of 1 John as John's 'catholic epistle'[31] – perhaps in contrast to 2 and 3 John, which are addressed to specified persons.[32] Later, however, 2 and 3 John were also reckoned among the seven Catholic Epistles (James, 1 and 2 Peter, 1, 2 and 3 John, Jude);[33] in this broader sense the term 'catholic' meant more or less 'canonical'[34] – canonical, that is to say, in addition to the Pauline epistles.

All three epistles are included in Athanasius's list of twenty-seven New Testament books issued in AD 367, and in the similar lists approved by the Councils of Hippo (393) and Carthage (397).

III BIBLIOGRAPHY

Among the numerous expositions of these Epistles there are seven which I have found outstandingly useful:

B. F. Westcott, *The Epistles of St. John* (London, first edition, 1883; fourth edition, 1902). This commentary, based on the Greek text, was reissued in 1966 by the Marcham Manor Press, Abingdon, Berkshire.

G. G. Findlay, *Fellowship in the Life Eternal* (London, 1909).

R. Law, *The Tests of Life* (Edinburgh, first edition, 1909; third edition, 1914). This study, described by A. M. Hunter as 'a liberal education in Biblical theology', was reissued in 1968 by the Baker Book House, Grand Rapids, Michigan, in their 'Limited Editions Library'.

A. E. Brooke, *The Johannine Epistles*. International Critical Commentary (Edinburgh, 1912). Based on the Greek text.

C. H. Dodd, *The Johannine Epistles*. Moffatt New Testament Commentary (London, 1946). Based, like all the volumes in the same series, on James Moffatt's translation.

R. Schnackenburg, *Die Johannesbriefe*. Herder's Theological Commentary on the NT (Freiburg, third edition, 1965).

R. Bultmann, *The Johannine Epistles*. Hermeneia (Philadelphia, 1973).

J. L. Houlden, *A Commentary on the Johannine Epistles*. Black's New Testament Commentaries (London, 1973).

Among shorter and more popular commentaries these are worthy of special mention:

N. Alexander, *The Epistles of John*, Torch Commentaries (London, 1962).

J. R. W. Stott, *The Epistles of John*, Tyndale NT Commentaries (London, 1964).

R. R. Williams, *The Letters of John and James*, Cambridge Bible Commentary on the New English Bible (Cambridge, 1965).

Other works containing material relevant to the study of the three Epistles are:

O. Cullmann, *The Early Church* (London, 1956).

W. F. Howard, *Christianity according to St. John* (London, 1943).

T. W. Manson, *On Paul and John* (London, 1963).

W. Nauck, *Die Tradition und der Charakter des ersten Johannesbriefes* (Tübingen, 1957).

Further important contributions to their study, especially in the form of periodical or occasional articles, are mentioned in footnotes.

NOTES

1. Although the apostles are not referred to as such in either the Gospel or the Epistles of John. this commentary uses the terminology 'the apostolic (*or* the apostles') teaching, fellowship *or* tradition' to denote what John prefers to call 'that was from the beginning' (see notes on 1. 1; 2. 7, 24).

2. Polycrates, bishop of Ephesus, writing to Victor, bishop of Rome *c*. AD 190, mentions among the 'great luminaries' who died and were buried in proconsular Asia Philip and two of his daughters (whose graves were in Hierapolis) and a third daughter (whose grave was in Ephesus), 'and John, who leaned on the Lord's breast, who was a priest wearing the *petalon*, a martyr and teacher; he also sleeps in Ephesus' (quoted by Eusebius, *Hist. Eccl.* iii. 31. 3; v. 24. 2). The *petalon* was the inscribed plate of gold attached to the high-priestly mitre or turban; Polycrates's language about it is best understood figuratively. Polycrates appears to have confused Philip the

apostle with Philip the evangelist; his contemporary, the Phrygian Montanist Proclus, points clearly to the Philip of Acts 21. 8 f. when he says in his correspondence with Gaius, a Roman presbyter, that 'the four daughters of Philip, who were prophetesses, were at Hierapolis in Asia; their grave is there and so is their father's' (quoted by Eusebius, *Hist. Eccl.* iii. 31. 4). About the same time Irenaeus, bishop of Lyons, states that 'John the disciple of the Lord, who leaned on His breast, himself also published the Gospel while he stayed at Ephesus in Asia' (*Against Heresies* iii. 1. 1). In the time of Dionysius, bishop of Alexandria (*c*. AD 270), two places were pointed out at Ephesus as the site of John's tomb (Eusebius, *Hist. Eccl.* vii. 25. 16).

3. Identified in John 21. 20–24 with 'the disciple whom Jesus loved'; cf. also John 13. 23 ff. (where this disciple is described as 'lying close to the breast of Jesus' at the Last Supper); 19. 26 f. (where he stands near the cross); 20. 2 ff., where he is convinced by the silent witness of the empty tomb); 21. 7 (where he recognizes the risen Lord). See also pp. 135 f.

4. From Irenaeus's letter to Florinus, in which he goes on to remind his former companion how Polycarp recalled 'the things concerning the Lord which he had heard from them, His miracles and His teaching, and how Polycarp had received them from eye-witnesses of the Word of life and reported all things in accordance with the Scriptures' (quoted by Eusebius, *Hist. Eccl.* v. 20. 6). Similarly, in his letter to Victor of Rome on the proper date of Easter, Irenaeus affirms that Polycarp had always followed the quartodeciman dating (i.e. he observed Passover on Nisan 14, after the Jewish precedent, irrespective of the weekday on which it fell) 'in company with John the disciple of our Lord and the other apostles with whom he associated' (quoted by Eusebius, *Hist. Eccl.* v. 24. 16). The absence of any reference to John in Pionius's later *Life of Polycarp* (*c*. AD 250) does not weaken the testimony of Irenaeus; Pionius's strong anti-quartodeciman convictions would be sufficient to dictate silence about John, who was regarded as the greatest authority for quartodeciman practice.

5. From his *Exegesis of the Dominical Oracles*, a work in five books now extant only in fragments quoted by later Christian writers, several of them by Eusebius, like the present one (*Hist. Eccl.* iii. 39. 4). Among those about whose testimony he sought information he mentions 'John' in a list of 'disciples of the Lord' in the past tense, and 'the elder John' as one of two 'disciples of the Lord' in the present tense (see the whole quotation on p. 136). If he means to distinguish two men called John, the former being presumably the apostle, the question arises whether 'John the disciple of the Lord' referred to by other Asian writers should be identified with the apostle or with 'the elder John'. This question remains unresolved; it was discussed by Dionysius of Alexandria in his day and by Eusebius fifty years later (*Hist. Eccl.* vii. 25. 6–27). The late fourth-century *Apostolic Constitutions* gives a list of bishops alleged to have been appointed to their sees by apostles, including 'in Ephesus, . . . John appointed by me John' (vii. 46). The independent value of this list is negligible, but it probably does bear witness to the tradition of two Johns at Ephesus, as does also a treatise (implausibly ascribed to Eusebius) found in some manuscripts of the Syriac Peshitta version, which mentions among three disciples of John the Evangelist 'John, to whom he committed the presbyterate and the episcopal see after him'.

Irenaeus had no doubt that Papias was 'a hearer of John and a companion of Polycarp' (*Against Heresies* v. 33. 4); Eusebius, on the other hand, thinks that Papias makes it plain that, while he had heard Aristion and the elder

John, 'he had by no means been a hearer and eyewitness of the holy apostles' (*Hist. Eccl.* iii. 39. 2, 7). But Eusebius was anxious that no suspicion of apostolic authority should attach to Papias's millenarian views, of which he disapproved. The anti-Marcionite prologue to the Fourth Gospel, extant only in a corrupt Latin translation of the Greek original (which may be dated *c.* AD 175), seems to confirm Irenaeus's testimony: 'The Gospel of John was published and given to the churches by John while he was yet in the body, as a man of Hierapolis, Papias by name, John's dear disciple, has related in his five exegetical books' (the adjective 'exegetical' is a highly probable emendation).

Several legends about John were preserved in Ephesus and its neighbourhood, including one about a former disciple of his who became a brigand chief and was sought out by John and restored to Christian fellowship (Clement of Alexandria, *Who is the rich man who is saved?* 42, quoted also by Eusebius, *Hist. Eccl.* iii. 23. 5–19), and another to the effect that in extreme old age, when he was taken to meet fellow-Christians, all he could do was to sum up the burden of his ministry by repeating the admonition: 'Little children, love one another' (Jerome, *Commentary on Galatians* 6. 10). No historical worth attaches to the apocryphal *Acts of John* (*c.* AD 160).

6. From Gr. *dokein*, 'to seem'. Cf. Ignatius, *To the Smyrnaeans* 2, where, after affirming his faith in Jesus incarnate, crucified and risen, he says: 'He suffered all these things for us that we might be saved; and he truly suffered, even as he truly raised himself – not, as some unbelievers say, that he *seemed* to have suffered' (where the repeated 'truly' is set in antithesis to mere *seeming*); similarly *To the Trallians* 10.

7. From Gr. *dēmiourgos*, literally 'public workman' (*dēmio-ergos*), 'artisan'; it is the word used of God in Heb. 11. 10 (but not in a dualistic or gnostic sense) and translated 'maker' in AV, RV and RSV (NEB 'builder').

8. The Christianity with which Muhammad became acquainted in his early days appears to have been docetic in outlook; hence the statement in the *Qur'ān* (4. 157): 'they did not kill him and did not crucify him, but he was counterfeited for them' (i.e. it was an effigy or simulacrum of Jesus that was fastened to the cross).

9. As in the legend about John's leaving the public baths at Ephesus in precipitate haste when he heard on one occasion that Cerinthus had entered: 'Let us flee, lest the baths fall in while Cerinthus, the enemy of the truth, is within' (related by Irenaeus, *Against Heresies* iii. 3. 4, as a story told by Polycarp).

10. Irenaeus, *Against Heresies* i. 26. 1. Gaius of Rome, contemporary with Irenaeus, charged Cerinthus with teaching that the marriage supper of the Lamb would last on earth for a thousand years, and indeed held that the Johannine Apocalypse was the work of Cerinthus. Dionysius of Alexandria also ascribed millenarian views to Cerinthus (both Gaius and Dionysius are quoted to this effect by Eusebius, *Hist. Eccl.* iii. 28. 1–5; cf. vii. 25. 1–3).

11. R. M. Grant (*A Historical Introduction to the NT*, London, 1963, p. 233) thinks that John might have in mind the views of Menander of Antioch, a follower (it is said) of Simon Magus (his views are summarized by Irenaeus, *Against Heresies* i. 23. 5).

12. 'John conducts himself with the independence and sovereignty of one who was in a position to say: *La tradition, c'est moi!*' (P. H. Menoud, *L'évangile de Jean d'après les recherches récentes*, Neuchatel & Paris, 1947, p. 77).

13. Cf. C. H. Dodd, *Historical Tradition in the Fourth Gospel* (Cambridge, 1963);

J. A. T. Robinson, 'The New Look on the Fourth Gospel', in *Twelve NT Studies*, London, 1962, pp. 94 ff., an essay which ends with the words: 'The decisive question is the status and origin of the Johannine tradition. Did this come out of the blue round about the year AD 100? Or is there a real continuity, not merely in the memory of one old man, but in the life of an on-going community, with the earliest days of Christianity? What, I think, fundamentally distinguishes the "new look" on the fourth Gospel is that it answers that question in the affirmative. But if we do assert this continuity, it is obviously going at one and the same time to reduce the necessity for making everything depend upon apostolic authorship *and* to make us very much more open to its possibility' (p. 106). The Johannine Epistles, it may be said, provide us with living evidence for the maintenance of the tradition both 'in the memory of one old man' (the Elder) and 'in the life of an on-going community' (the companies addressed and referred to as adhering to what they had heard 'from the beginning').

14. Cf. O. Cullmann, 'The Tradition', in *The Early Church* (London, 1956), pp. 59 ff.
15. *To the Ephesians* 7. 2. Cf. also John 1. 14; 2 John 7. Ignatius does not hesitate to speak of Jesus as God.
16. Every one who does not confess that Jesus Christ has come in the flesh is Antichrist' (*To the Philippians* 7. 1). Cf. 2 John 7. See p. 72.
17. Eusebius, *Hist. Eccl.* iii. 39. 17.
18. Possible traces in the Valentinian *Gospel of Truth* (*c.* AD 140) are 'the Father knows all things' (27. 24; cf. 1 John 3. 20) and 'he came forth in flesh' (31. 4 f.; cf. 1 John 4. 2 f.).
19. Justin's statement that 'we are called God's trueborn children, and so we are, if we keep his commandments' (*Dialogue with Trypho* 123. 9) looks very much like a reminiscence of 1 John 3. 1, coupled with 2. 3.
20. Compare, e.g., 'how greatly will you love Him who so loved you first?' (*Diogn.* 10. 3) with 1 John 4. 19.
21. E.g. *Against Heresies* iii. 16. 5.
22. E.g. *Against Marcion* v. 16.
23. Lines 26–34.
24. Lines 68 f. For practical purposes *in catholica* may be translated 'in the canon'.
25. So P. Katz, 'The Johannine Epistles in the Muratorian Canon', *JTS* n.s. 8 (1957), pp. 273 f.
26. Cf. A. Harnack, *Zur Revision der Prinzipien der neutestamentlichen Textkritik* (Leipzig, 1916), pp. 61 f.; T. W. Manson, 'The Johannine Epistles and the Canon of the NT', *JTS* 48 (1947), pp. 32 f.
27. *Miscellanies* ii. 15. 66; *Adumbrations* iv. 437, etc.
28. Quoted by Eusebius, *Hist. Eccl.* vi. 25. 10.
29. *Hist. Eccl.* iii. 24. 17 f.
30. *Commentary on Matthew*, xvii. 19.
31. Quoted by Eusebius, *Hist. Eccl.* vii. 25. 7, 10.
32. Cf. Eusebius, *Hist. Eccl.* vii. 25. 11.
33. Eusebius refers to the seven epistles 'called catholic' (*Hist. Eccl.* ii. 23. 25).
34. In this sense Jerome sometimes renders Gr. *katholikos* by Lat. *catholicus*, sometimes by *canonicus*.

THE FIRST EPISTLE OF JOHN

1 *Character and Purpose*

The First Epistle of John neither begins nor ends like an epistle; it does not start with any indication of the identity of the writer or of the people whom he addresses,[1] nor does it end with personal greetings. In form and content it is a message of encouragement and reassurance, sent to a group of Christians who were perplexed and bewildered by recent happenings in their midst. We cannot be sure whether it was sent to a single church or to several churches in an area; what is reasonably certain is that the recipients lived in some district of the province of Asia, and that shortly before the sending of this message some of their most talented brethren had left them in order to form a new community or communities devoted to a specially attractive line of teaching which was represented as an advance on anything that Christians had been taught thus far. When we say it was specially attractive, we mean that it was specially attractive to people of some intellectual attainment. For the ordinary rank and file of Christians it had less appeal; indeed, it was not intended for them, but rather for an élite of spiritual initiates. It deviated from the teaching which had previously been current among the churches of Asia in theory and practice alike.

In its theory it closely resembled the docetic brand of Gnosticism; in particular, it denied that Jesus Christ had 'come in the flesh' (1 John 4. 2 f.). In the particular climate of opinion to which this teaching owed its existence, 'thoughtful men' could not be expected to believe in the 'crude' incarnationalism of the primitive message; it was a relief to have a re-statement of Christianity presented to them which did not compel them to be obscurantists or to keep different areas of knowledge in watertight compartments.

The re-stating of the gospel is a necessary task which must

engage the serious concern of those who wish to commend it to their fellows in each succeeding generation. In the first Christian century no one played a more conspicuous or successful part in re-stating the gospel than John himself did. A comparison of the Synoptic Gospels with the Fourth Gospel makes it plain that in the latter the message of the former has been transposed into a different key. Yet the message which John thus transposes or re-states is the same essential message as that of the earlier Evangelists, but presented in an idiom which was more intelligible to Hellenistic readers in the eastern Mediterranean two generations after the saving events had taken place – in an idiom which was calculated to bring out the eternal validity of those events, and which in fact continues even in our day to bring out their eternal validity. There can be a true re-statement of the gospel as there can be a false one; everything depends on whether the essence of the gospel is preserved or lost in the re-statement. Since the incarnation of the Son of God is of the abiding essence of the gospel, the Cerinthian re-statement or anything of the same general character could not be accepted as truly Christian.

On the practical level these new teachers claimed to have reached such an advanced stage in spiritual experience that they were 'beyond good and evil'. They maintained that they had no sin, not in the sense that they had attained moral perfection but in the sense that what might be sin for people at a less mature stage of inner development was no longer sin for the completely 'spiritual' man. For him ethical distinctions had ceased to be relevant. Perhaps he called them 'merely' ethical distinctions. (Christians stand on the brink of disaster when they begin to modify the adjective 'ethical' with the adverb 'merely'.) The new teaching thus combined a new theology with a new morality.

Neither theology nor morality is necessarily the worse for being 'new'. When our Lord began His public ministry in Galilee His hearers recognized that what He brought was 'a new teaching' (Mark 1. 27); and those who listened to the Sermon on the Mount were aware that they were being presented with a 'new morality', for all our Lord's claim that He was but reaffirming the essence of the law and the prophets, 'for he taught them as one who had authority, and not as their scribes' (Matt. 7. 29). The question to be asked of all teaching is not 'Is it new?' but 'Is it true?' When this latter question was put to the new teaching with which John takes issue, the answer was that it was not true. It could not be, for it was at variance with the truth incarnate in Jesus; far from bringing out the deeper implications of the gospel, it utterly subverted it. No appeal to the principle of complementarity could reconcile the one to the other.

In such a situation it was impossible for those who propagated and embraced the new teaching to continue with those who believed that the old was better. In doctrine and practice alike the two were so incompatible that their respective supporters had to part company. The new teachers led their followers out from the fellowship of those who refused to go along with their teaching; they probably accused those who adhered to the old ways of shutting their eyes to the light, if not of committing the sin against the Holy Spirit.

The Christians who remained in their former fellowship were hard hit and shaken by the secession of these others, and needed to be reassured. The others were so confident that they were right; they talked in such superior terms of their special initiation into the true knowledge that humbler believers might well wonder whether their foundation was so secure as they had thought. Where did the truth lie? Where was eternal life to be found? In their old fellowship, or with the seceders? The seceders probably said, 'We've got it; you haven't!' How could it be known which side was right? What were the criteria?

To Christians in this perplexity, then, the First Epistle of John was written. The writer was in the best possible position to state the criteria of truth and life, and to help his readers to see that they, and not the seceders, satisfied these criteria. 'I write this', he says, 'to you who believe in the name of the Son of God, that you may know that you have eternal life' (1 John 5. 13).

Here is a man who knows what he is talking about. He knows what the true gospel is, because he was there when it began. He had been a companion of the incarnate Word of Life – had seen Him, heard Him, touched Him. His readers had not had this experience, but he writes to share with them what he and his fellow-disciples experienced. Thus 'the Elder' (as he was called *par excellence* in his circle of friends) and his 'little children' would rejoice together in the certainty which he possessed already and which, imparted by him to them, would banish their bewilderment and doubt.

The doctrinal basis of the epistle is the common stock of apostolic Christianity, the *kērygma* ('preaching') and *didachē* ('teaching') of which appear here as 'the witness' and 'the commandment'. The 'witness' proclaims the love of God in the sacrifice of Christ; the 'commandment' applies the practical implication of the 'witness' to the lives of believers.[2]

Where is eternal life to be found? In the Son of God. 'God gave us eternal life, and this life is in His Son. He who has the Son has the life; he who has not the Son of God has not the life' (1 John 5. 11 f.). But the Son of God had become incarnate; those who denied His incarnation had not the Son, and therefore could not have that eternal life which was to be found only in Him. It was as simple as that.

John and his readers, who remained faithful to the original teaching and fellowship,[3] were in the sphere where eternal life might be enjoyed, because their fellowship was with the Father and with His Son Jesus Christ. Those who turned their backs on this fellowship turned their backs on eternal life. They might claim to possess it – indeed, they might claim to be in exclusive possession of it – but their claim was vain. They had abandoned the true foundation. So, John exhorts his readers, 'let what you heard from the beginning abide in you. If what you heard from the beginning abides in you, then you will abide in the Son and in the Father' (1 John 2. 24).

In these words, John makes a solemn affirmation of the permanent validity of the apostolic witness to Christ. For us, that witness is enshrined in the New Testament writings, our rule of faith and practice. We may transpose, re-state, re-translate as much as we will; only let us see to it that our transposition, re-statement and re-translation make the apostolic witness clearer than ever, rather than obscure it or dilute it or turn it into some-thing else. 'For no other foundation can any one lay than that which is laid, which is Jesus Christ' (1 Cor. 3. 11). It is not for nothing that the heading of 1 John in the New English Bible is 'Recall to Fundamentals'.

2 *Structure and Authorship*

Attempts to trace a consecutive argument throughout 1 John have never succeeded. For the convenience of a commentator and his readers, it is possible to present such an analysis of the epistle as is given on pp. 31 f., but this does not imply that the author himself worked to an organized plan. At best we can distinguish three main courses of thought: the first (1. 5–2. 27), which has two main themes, ethical (walking in light) and Christological (confessing Jesus as the Christ); the second (2. 28–4. 6), which repeats the ethical and Christological themes with variations; the third (4. 7–5. 12), where the same two essential themes are presented as love and faith and shown to be inseparable and indispensable products of life in Christ.[4]

If attempts to trace a consecutive argument have not been successful, attempts to distinguish sources have been even less so. It is plain to the observant reader that we have here passages in homiletic style interspersed with epigrammatic theses, often grouped in antithetic pairs. We may think of the repeated 'If we say . . .' of 1. 6 ff., 'He who says . . .' of 2. 4 ff., or the four pairs of antitheses in 2. 28–3. 10.[5] Rudolf Bultmann has discerned twenty-six antithetical couplets (closely related in his mind to the 'revelation discourses' of the Fourth Gospel), which he regards as the core of the epistle, worked over in homiletic fashion by another author, to whom we owe the epistle in its present form.[6] Wolfgang Nauck similarly distinguishes the antithetical core from the revised and enlarged document, but ascribes both parts of the work to the same hand.[7] It is unlikely, however, that the antitheses ever existed as a separate document; the author may well have used them in his oral ministry to drive home his message, and incorporates them at appropriate points in this written homily. Source criticism is as barren an exercise in the study of this epistle as it is in the study of the Fourth Gospel.[8]

The main question of authorship raised by the study of 1 John is whether it is the work of the Fourth Evangelist. To some students of the two compositions no such question arises.[9] Thus T. W. Manson, lecturing on Johannine theology, pointed out that this cannot be deduced with certainty from the Fourth Gospel, because of the difficulty of distinguishing the teaching of Jesus from the interpretation of the Evangelist; if we are to 'examine the Johannine theology in its relatively pure state', then 'the proper method is to begin with the Epistle and there find what are the leading theological ideas of the author'.[10] Many years previously another English writer, John Chapman, went so far as to say that 'no sane critic will deny that the Gospel and the first Epistle are from the same pen'.[11] In expressing himself thus, he presumably meant to exclude from the category of 'sane' critics certain continental scholars who had denied identity of authorship, but his prediction (whether it was intended as such or not) was falsified twenty-six years later when C. H. Dodd – a 'sane critic' if ever there was one – presented an argument for diversity of authorship, based partly on vocabulary and style and partly on theological outlook. He found the Epistle to be less Hebraic and Jewish than the Gospel and freer in its adoption of Hellenistic thought-forms and expressions, and in its theology – its doctrine of the atonement and the Paraclete, and especially its eschatology – to be nearer to popular Christianity than is the Gospel. Accordingly he gave up what he acknowledged to be 'the unvarying tradition from early times'.[12]

No one disputes the remarkably close relation between the two compositions in language and outlook; they clearly come from the same circle or school if not from the same individual. It is not easy to speak dogmatically about the common authorship of two anonymous works which, while exhibiting this close relation, belong to different literary genres. This last fact may account in large measure for the differences in vocabulary and style; as for the theological differences, these have been exaggerated. There is futurist as well as realized eschatology in the Fourth Gospel (cf. John 5. 28 f.; 6. 39 f., 44; 12. 48) and realized as well as futurist eschatology in the Epistle (e.g. the recognition of false teachers as 'antichrists' already present in 1 John 2. 18). Moreover, the 'notable differences between the Gospel and the Epistle turn out to be differences not between the Epistle and the Gospel as a whole, but between the Epistle and certain sections of the Gospel'[13] – those sections, more specifically, which are characterized by Aramaisms. On the whole, it cannot be said that the arguments for diversity of authorship are sufficient to overthrow the evidence, both internal and external, for common authorship.[14]

A date towards the end of the first century is most probable.[15] This is indicated by the type of heretical teaching against which the readers are put on their guard, and is confirmed by the evidence that the Epistle was known early in the second century – possibly by Ignatius and certainly by Polycarp and Papias.[16]

3 *Analysis of 1 John*

1 Prologue (1. 1–4)

2 Walking in Light (1. 5–2. 2)
   (*a*) The character of God (1. 5)
   (*b*) Three antithetic tests of life (1. 6–2. 2)

3 The New Commandment (2. 3–17)
   (*a*) The test of obedience (2. 3–6)
   (*b*) The test of love (2. 7–11)
   (*c*) Encouragement to three age-groups (2. 12–14)
   (*d*) Warning against the world (2. 15–17)

4 The Teaching of Antichrist (2. 18–27)
   (*a*) Many antichrists (2. 18)
   (*b*) The test of perseverance (2. 19)
   (*c*) Distinguishing truth and error (2. 20–27)

5 Children of God (2. 28–3. 24)
   (*a*) The two families (2. 28–3. 10)

NOTES

1. Augustine (*Questions on the Gospels* ii. 39) gives 1 John the title 'To the Parthians'; this title was first (mistakenly) attached to 2 John, and then in the course of transmission transferred to the beginning of the group of three epistles. See p. 145, n. 13.

2. See especially C. H. Dodd, *The Johannine Epistles* (London, 1946), pp. xxvii ff.

3. A detailed examination of the beliefs held in common by John and the readers of his first epistle is made by O. A. Piper, 'I John and the Didache of the Primitive Church', *JBL* 66 (1947), pp. 437 ff.

4. Here I follow rather closely W. G. Kümmel, *Introduction to the New Testament* (London, 1966), pp. 306 f.

5. See p. 78.

6. 'Analyse des ersten Johannesbriefes', *Festgabe für A. Jülicher* (Tübingen, 1927), pp. 138 ff. Later Bultmann argued for the further activity of an ecclesiastical redactor, who added an appendix (5. 14–21) and a few other passages propounding the church's eschatology and doctrine of atonement through the blood of Christ ('Die kirchliche Redaktion des ersten Johannesbriefes', *In memoriam E. Lohmeyer*, Stuttgart, 1951, pp. 181 ff.). Most recently, in his commentary, he has confirmed his continued adherence to these views, but supplemented them with the suggestion that 1 John 1. 5–2. 27 was a preliminary draft, and that the same themes as are handled in it are treated again in the individual literary units making up 2. 28–5. 12, in a modified and amplified but unconnected fashion (*The Johannine Epistles*, Philadelphia, 1973, p. 2).

7. *Die Tradition und der Charakter des ersten Johannesbriefes* (Tübingen, 1957), pp. 1 ff.

8. In *The Puzzle of 1 John* (London, 1966), J. C. O'Neill argues that the author of the epistle was a member of a Jewish sectarian group who, in common with the majority of his fellow-members, came to acknowledge Jesus as the Messiah. The epistle comprises twelve poetic admonitions belonging to the traditional literature of the group which he enlarged to show that the ideals of the group had been realized in Jesus. Those people whose views are controverted in the epistle are the members of the group who had refused to join in recognizing Jesus as the Messiah. The prologue (1. 1–4) is omitted from Dr. O'Neill's purview for purposes of this analysis.

9. Cf. B. F. Westcott: 'The arguments which have been alleged to support the opinion that the Books [the Fourth Gospel and the First Epistle] were by different authors, do not seem to me to need serious examination. They could not be urged if the books were not detached from life and criticised without regard to their main characteristics' (*The Epistles of St. John*, London, 1902, p. xxx, n. 1).

10. *On Paul and John* (London, 1963), pp. 87 f.

11. *John the Presbyter and the Fourth Gospel* (Oxford, 1911), p. 72.

12. 'The First Epistle of John and the Fourth Gospel', *BJRL* 21 (1937), pp. 129 ff.; cf. also his *The Johannine Epistles* (London, 1946), pp. xlvii ff. In particular, his conclusions were influenced by the contrast he saw between the realized eschatology of the Gospel and the futurist eschatology of the Epistle.

13. T. W. Manson, *On Paul and John*, pp. 86 ff.; see also his *Studies in the Gospels and Epistles* (Manchester, 1962), pp. 116 f.

14. Detailed arguments for common authorship, marshalled with C. H. Dodd's arguments for diversity of authorship in mind, are most cogently presented by W. F. Howard in 'The Common Authorship of the Johannine Gospel and Epistles', *JTS* 48 (1947), pp. 12 ff., reprinted in *The Fourth Gospel in Recent Criticism and Interpretation*[4] (London, 1955), pp. 282 ff.

15. The same approximate date is indicated for the Gospel, but which of the two was earlier or later cannot be determined.

16. See p. 18.

TEXT AND EXPOSITION

CHAPTER I

1 PROLOGUE (1. 1–4)

V. 1   That which was from the beginning, that which we have heard, that which we have seen with our eyes, that which we beheld, and our hands handled, concerning the [1]Word of life (v. 2 and the life was manifested, and we have seen, and bear witness, and declare unto you the life, the eternal *life*, which was with the Father, and was manifested unto us); v. 3 that which we have seen and heard declare we unto you also, that ye also may have fellowship with us:

[1] Or, *word*.

The structure of the sentence covering the first two and a half verses of chapter 1 (with the parenthesis in verse 2) is unusually complicated for the Johannine writings, and an English version will be more readily intelligible if it takes four sentences to say what the Greek text says in one:

> Our theme is that which was from the beginning, which we have heard, which we have seen with our eyes, which we beheld and our hands handled. Our theme, in short, concerns the word of Life – that Life which was made manifest. Yes, we have seen and we bear witness; we make known to you the Eternal Life which was with the Father and was made manifest to us. What we have seen and heard we make known to you also, in order that you in your turn may have fellowship with us.

The opening words of the epistle, 'that which was from the beginning (Gr. *ap' archēs*)', resemble the opening words of the Gospel of John, 'In the beginning (*en archē*) was the Word'. It is not necessary, however, to conclude that the two 'beginnings' are identical; more probably they are not. The 'beginning' of John 1. 1 is the beginning of time, the 'beginning' of Gen. 1. 1, in which God created the heaven and the earth. At that time, says the Evangelist, when the material universe came into being, the Word already existed. The world had a beginning, but the Word had none.[1] The phrase 'from the beginning' in 1 John 1. 1 is best understood in the sense which it occasionally bears later in the epistle: for example, in 1 John 2. 7, where John reminds his readers of the 'old commandment which you had *from the beginning*', and in 1 John 2. 24, where he urges them to adhere to 'what you heard *from the beginning*'.[2] The 'beginning' in this sense is the beginning of the gospel – in 1 John 2. 7, 24, the beginning of the gospel so far as their acquaintance with it was concerned, while in 1 John 1. 1 it is the beginning of the gospel absolutely, the beginning as it was known to one who was present at the time and directly witnessed the saving events. The neuter gender of 'that which was from the beginning' points to the gospel rather than to the personal Christ, although indeed the gospel is so completely bound up with the personal Christ that what is primarily true of the one may be said of the other. It was the personal Christ who was heard, seen and touched by John and his fellow-disciples, and if it is maintained that, despite the neuter gender of the relative pronoun, He is the one who is said to have been 'from the beginning', an analogy to this use of the phrase could also be found in chapter 2, where mention is made of God or Christ as 'him who is from the beginning' (verses 13, 14).

John's authority to speak about 'that which was from the beginning' is the authority of first-hand knowledge. He could be described, in Luke's language, as one of 'those who from the beginning (Gr. *ap' archēs*, as here) were eyewitnesses and ministers of the word' (Luke 1. 2). This, he says (including his fellow-disciples along with himself), is the reality 'which we have heard, . . . which we have seen with our eyes, . . . which we beheld, and our hands handled'.[3] They were the men to whom Jesus said, 'blessed are your eyes, for they see, and your ears, for they hear. Truly, I say to you, many prophets and righteous men longed to see what you see, and did not see it, and to hear what you hear, and did not hear it' (Matt. 13. 16, 17; cf. Luke 10. 23, 24). The language John uses is the language of apostolic witness: 'we cannot but speak of what we have seen and heard' was the reply

of the apostles Peter and John to the Sanhedrin when they were
ordered to give up speaking or teaching in Jesus' name (Acts 4. 20).
If we ask *who* it was that they heard and saw, the answer is that
they heard and saw Jesus; if we ask *what* it was, the answer is that
they heard His words and saw His works.

But in addition to seeing with the eyes, John speaks of 'that
which we beheld'. Here the Greek verb (*theaomai*) is the one used
in John 1. 14, where the Evangelist tells how, when the Eternal
Word became flesh and tabernacled among men, he and his
companions '*beheld* his glory'. So in the present passage the
implication of this rather 'elevated' verb of seeing may be that
they penetrated beyond what was accessible to outward vision to
discern the inward glory. And as for the further statement that
'our hands handled' the reality of which he speaks, it can hardly be
overlooked that this verb (Gr. *psēlaphaō*) is used in reference to
the risen Christ, not indeed in the Gospel of John (although the
Thomas incident of John 20. 24–29 springs to mind in this
connexion), but in Luke 24. 39, where the disciples, frightened at
the sudden appearance of the Risen One, are bidden: 'handle me,
and see; for a spirit has not flesh and bones as you see that I have'.[4]

From the compiler of the Muratorian canon[5] onwards, many
commentators have treated the eyewitness claim of these verses as
a reference to the contents of the Fourth Gospel, as though this
epistle were a covering note sent out with the Gospel and certifying
the authenticity of its record. But there is nothing in the present
context to suggest this; it is better to understand the eyewitness
claim as the author's way of emphasizing the authority with which
he writes on 'that which was from the beginning'.

'Our theme, in short, concerns the word of life.' These two
terms, 'word' (Gr. *logos*) and 'life' (Gr. *zōē*), are keywords of the
Gospel of John. Of the Eternal Word the Evangelist says, 'In him
was life, and the life was the light of men' (John 1. 4). But whereas
in the Prologue to the Gospel it is the term 'Word' rather than
'life' that is used personally of the One who was in the beginning
with God, here it is the term 'Life' rather than 'word' that is so
used. The 'word of life' is the message of life (that is, the gospel);

but the life which forms the subject-matter of that message is 'the eternal life, which was with the Father and was manifested to us'. If the Gospel speaks of the incarnation of the Eternal Word, the Epistle speaks of the manifestation of the Eternal Life. 'The Word was God', says the Gospel; 'this is the true God and eternal life', says the Epistle (1 John 5. 20). When it is said that the Eternal Life was 'with the Father', the same preposition (Gr. *pros*) is used as in the repeated statement of John 1. 1, 2, that the Word was *'with* God'. There is no theologically profound significance in the preposition itself, except as it borrows some such significance from its context; the same preposition is similarly used in a quite non-theological context when the people of Nazareth, astonished at the power and wisdom of their fellow-townsman Jesus, say 'are not his sisters here *with* us?' (Mark 6. 3).

This epistle, then, is justly called 'the epistle of eternal life'.[6] It shows how and in whom that life was uniquely and perfectly manifested; it shows how the presence of that life in men and women may be recognized. John's own experience of that life entitles him to speak of it with assurance and communicate his assurance to others: this, he says, we have seen; to this we bear witness; this we make known to you.

It has been argued that this language is not necessarily to be understood as the language of an eyewitness. Christians of every generation have entered into the fellowship of the first Christian generation, and take the language of its witness on their own lips:

> What we have seen and heard
> With confidence we tell.

So here, it may be said, the 'we' is the corporate 'we', just as a twentieth-century Englishman (recalling the death of Joan of Arc in 1431) can speak of

> That old, undying sin we shared
> In Rouen market-place

or just as in Amos 2. 10, half a millennium after the Exodus, the corporate 'you' is used in God's words to the Israelites: 'I brought you up out of the land of Egypt, and led you forty years in the wilderness'.[7]

But the antithesis between 'we' and 'you' in 1 John 1. 3 makes this interpretation improbable. John tells his fellow-Christians to whom he writes of what he and his contemporaries had seen and heard, because his readers had *not* seen and heard it. We must sometimes distinguish between the *inclusive* 'we' (meaning 'you and I' or 'you and we') and the *exclusive* 'we' (meaning 'we and not you'); and in 1 John 1. 3 'we' is exclusive: *we* had this experience, *you* did not have it, but *we* are sharing it with *you* in order that *you* may share it with *us* – 'in order that you in your turn may have fellowship with us'. This language is most naturally understood if a surviving member of the first Christian generation is addressing members of a later Christian generation, who could not have that unmediated contact with the beginning of the gospel that he himself had. (We should compare the inclusion in the dominical petition of John 17. 20 of the next generation which will believe through the original disciples' witness.)

But the implications of their sharing what John had to impart to them were more far-reaching than they might have expected. They were called to follow the steps of their predecessors who, after the first Christian Pentecost, 'devoted themselves to the apostles' teaching and fellowship' (Acts 2. 42); and they were to learn that perseverance in the apostolic fellowship[8] involved fellowship with more than the apostles and their successors.

V. 3b yea, and our fellowship is with the Father, and with his Son Jesus Christ:

John desires his readers to have fellowship with himself and his associates by sharing their experience of the manifested life; but fellowship with John and his associates meant at the same time fellowship with the Father and with the Son. The word 'fellowship' (*koinōnia*) and its cognates are absent from the Gospel of John, but the idea which they express is not absent. It is present in Jesus' words to Peter, 'if I do not wash you, you have no part with me'

(John 13. 8);⁹ it is present in the parable of the Vine and the Branches (John 15. 1-16). It is present in Jesus' prayer for the disciples: 'as thou, Father, art in me, and I in thee, that they also may be in us, . . . I in them and thou in me, that they may become perfectly one' (John 17. 21, 23). It is present also in a form which comes quite close to what John says here in Jesus' answer to Judas (not Iscariot) in John 14. 23: 'If a man loves me, he will keep my words, and my Father will love him, and we will come to him and make our home with him'. True believers are those who dwell in Christ – that is to say, in the fellowship which embraces all the members of Christ. Since the apostles were the first to enter this fellowship, any one who adhered to the apostles' fellowship had, by that token, fellowship with Christ. And since Christ is the Son of God in whom the Father dwells (John 14. 10) and who in turn dwells in the Father's love (John 15. 10), so those who dwell in Him dwell in the Father (1 John 2. 24) – in other words, those who have fellowship with Him have fellowship with the Father through Him. There is nothing vague or merely sentimental about this fellowship; it involves obedience to the commandments of Christ and faithfulness to His teaching communicated through His apostles. Those who abandoned the apostolic teaching and fellowship severed themselves from fellowship with the Father and the Son.

Nothing is said here of the part played by the Spirit in this fellowship; but elsewhere in the epistle it is made plain that those to whom the Spirit of Christ has been given know by that fact that they dwell in Christ and He in them (1 John 3. 24; 4. 13). For Christian fellowship, in Paul's language, is the 'fellowship of the Spirit' (2 Cor. 13. 14; Phil. 2. 1); it is the fellowship into which believers are introduced and in which they are maintained by the indwelling Spirit of Christ.

V. 4 **and these things we write, that ¹our joy may be fulfilled.**

¹ Many ancient authorities read *your*.

There are two textual variants in this verse: the bulk of later manuscripts read 'to you' (*hymin*) in place of the emphatic 'we' (*hēmeis*) of the first clause (meaning 'we as distinct from you'), and 'your' (*hymōn*) in place of 'our' (*hēmōn*) in the second clause.[10] Neither of these variants is important. If 'to you' is not expressed in the first clause, it is in any case implied; and if 'our' is the possessive pronoun in the second clause, it is the inclusive 'our' (meaning 'our joy and yours together'), not the exclusive ('our joy, not yours'). John certainly sought his readers' joy, but their joy would be his, and that joy would be filled brimfull if they were firmly established in Christian faith and fellowship. The same theme of fulness of joy appears in the upper room discourses (John 15. 11; 16. 24).

2 WALKING IN LIGHT (1. 5–2. 2)

(*a*) *The Character of God* (1. 5)

If they are to have fellowship with the Father and with the Son, they must know the character of the God who has called them into fellowship with Himself.

V. 5 And this is the message which we have heard from him, and announce unto you, that God is light, and in him is no darkness at all.

Light in Gen. 1. 3 is the beginning of God's creation. In Ps. 104. 2 it is God's garment-like covering.[11] The light of God is frequently found as a metaphor for the life or salvation that He imparts: 'in thy light do we see light' (Ps. 36. 9) has as its parallel clause 'with thee is the fountain of life'. When, by a bolder use of metaphor, God Himself is described as light in the Old Testament, the intention is the same: 'The LORD is my light and my salvation' (Ps. 27. 1) stands in synonymous parallelism with 'The LORD is the stronghold of my life'. Similarly, when the Servant of the Lord is given 'as a light to the nations' in Isa. 49. 6, the purpose is, in God's words, 'that my salvation may reach to the end of the earth'.

So, in the prologue of John's Gospel the Eternal Word is 'the true light that enlightens every man' (John 1. 9); it is the life that resides in the Word that is 'the light of men' (John 1. 4). In the body of the Gospel Jesus accordingly says: 'I am the light of the world; he who follows me will not walk in darkness, but will have the light of life'[12] (John 8. 12). While life is the central thought in this use of 'light', however, there is in this Gospel the further thought of the spiritual illumination which comes when God reveals Himself in His Word, and this carries an ethical emphasis with it. If, despite the entry of the true light into the world, men love darkness rather than light, it is because their deeds are evil (John 3. 19–21); Jesus, in His final utterance to the Jewish public during Holy Week, urges them to believe in Him and so become 'sons of light', else the darkness will overtake them (John 12. 35 f., 46). This ethical sense of 'light' appears elsewhere in the New Testament, especially in Ephesians 5. 8–14, where the readers, who were once 'darkness' but are now 'light' in the Lord, are encouraged to live as 'children of light' and bring forth the 'fruit of light' rather than participate in the 'unfruitful works of darkness'. Outside the New Testament, the ethical use of the terms 'light' and 'darkness' is specially marked in the Qumran literature, where men are ruled either by the Prince of Light or by the Angel of Darkness, and practise truth and righteousness or falsehood and iniquity accordingly.[13] Such phraseology plays a prominent part in the series of affinities of concept and language which have been traced between the Qumran literature and the Johannine writings.

It is in the ethical sense that John here affirms that 'God is light, and in him is no darkness at all'. God, that is to say, is the source and essence of holiness and righteousness, goodness and truth; in Him there is nothing that is unholy or unrighteous, evil or false. He revealed Himself thus in the age of preparation before Christ came, and when the age of fulfilment dawned in Christ, this was the character of God as unveiled in the life that was the light of men. This being so, those whose 'fellowship is with the Father and with his Son Jesus Christ' will in their lives reflect the character of God; they will 'walk as children of light'.[14] Here, then, the first of a series of 'tests of life' is laid down.

(b) Three antithetic tests of life (1. 6–2. 2)

V. 6 If we say that we have fellowship with him, and walk in the darkness, we lie, and do not the truth:

Three tests are here laid down in the form of a false claim introduced by the clause 'if we say', each of these false claims being followed by the truth which is its antidote. The first of the three false claims is the claim to have fellowship with God at the same time as one's life is marked by unrighteousness. 'He who does what is true comes to the light, that it may be clearly seen that his deeds have been wrought in God' (John 3. 21); but 'every one who does evil hates the light, and does not come to the light, lest his deeds should be exposed' (John 3. 20). It may well be that the false teachers against whom John puts his readers on their guard were wide open to criticism in this respect, but it is equally necessary for those who adhere to the apostolic teaching and fellowship to be reminded that orthodoxy of doctrine is no substitute for righteousness of life. 'Truth in the inward being' (Ps. 51. 6) is what God desires in His people, and where that is present, it will manifest itself in all the ways of life.

This ethical use of the verb 'to walk' (*peripateō*) in the New Testament is particularly common in the Pauline letters but is also characteristic of these three Johannine letters, especially when we consider their brevity (cf., in addition to verses 6 and 7 here, 1 John 2. 6, 11; 2 John 4, 6; 3 John 3, 4). Similar language occurs in the Qumran texts; for example, the 'sons of righteousness' are said to 'walk in the ways of light' while the 'sons of wickedness' 'walk in the ways of darkness'.[15] In the Gospel of John there are a few passages which mark a transition from the literal sense of the verb to its denoting one's manner of life; Jesus says, for instance, 'If any one walks in the day, he does not stumble, because he sees the light of this world; but if any one walks in the night, he stumbles, because the light is not in him' (John 11. 9 f.); and again, 'Walk while you have the light, lest the darkness overtake you; he who walks in the darkness does not know where he goes. While you have the light, believe in the light, that you may become sons of light' (John 12. 35 f.).[16]

V. 7   but if we walk in the light, as he is in the light, we have fellowship one with another, and the blood of Jesus his Son cleanseth us from all sin.

Those who walk in the darkness do not know where they are going and cannot co-ordinate their courses; they stumble against one another and fall into confusion. On the other hand, those who walk in the light can see one another and avoid such clashes. Where spiritual light is concerned, much more than this can be said: those whose environment is that light in which God dwells are not only preserved from getting in one another's way, but actively and positively they enjoy fellowship one with another because each enjoys fellowship with God Himself.[17] This is the antithesis to the evil conduct and false claim which John has just exposed. The children of light are those whose behaviour reflects the character of God; they share with one another the fellowship which each enjoys 'with the Father and with his Son Jesus Christ'. By contrast, those who have opted out of this divine fellowship have abandoned the realm of light. Most serious of all the consequences of their apostasy is this: the blood of Jesus, which is constantly accessible for the cleansing[18] of those who remain within the fellowship, is not available for those who show a persistent preference for 'walking in darkness'.

The statement that 'the blood of Jesus . . . cleanseth us from all sin' (1. 7) is the subject of an 'Additional Note' in B. F. Westcott's commentary, entitled 'The idea of Christ's Blood in the New Testament', in which it is argued that the significance of blood in sacrifice is not restricted to the laying down of life but embraces 'the thought of the life preserved and active beyond death'.[19] Westcott expresses his indebtedness to an extended note in William Milligan's Croall Lectures for 1879–80, in which the classical passage on this subject, Lev. 17. 11, is taken to mean that the blood sprinkled on the altar is still 'a living thing, brought into the most intimate relation with the grace of God in its greatest potency'.[20] This interpretation of the shedding of the blood to mean the *release* of life rather than the sacrifice of life is open to criticism.[21] What John has in mind here is that cleansing of the conscience from guilt and moral defilement which is so insisted on in the Epistle to the Hebrews,[22] and which takes a leading place among the saving benefits of the redemptive self-sacrifice of Christ. These saving benefits are permanently available to those who are united to Christ, but not to those who sever themselves from Him. To be severed from the fellowship of Christ's people is to be severed from the fellowship of Christ Himself, so closely are He and His people joined.

V. 8   If we say that we have no sin, we deceive ourselves, and the truth is not in us.

But, say some of those against whom John's polemic is directed, what is it to us if the blood of Jesus is not available to cleanse us from sin? We have no sin! Here is the second false claim in the present series. If people claim – perhaps on the ground of their possession of the Spirit[23] – to have got beyond good and evil, to have reached a stage of spiritual development where moral principles are no longer relevant, they are self-deceived. The words 'the truth is not in us' are reminiscent of what is said of the devil in John 8. 44, 'there is no truth in him'. Those in whom the truth resides – and we may recall that in the Johannine writings the truth is embodied in Christ (John 14. 6) – will exhibit it in their lives; they will *practise* the truth (verse 6).

V. 9   If we confess our sins, he is faithful and righteous to forgive us our sins, and to cleanse us from all unrighteousness.

Here is the antidote to the second false claim: those who deny their sin will feel no need of recourse to the cleansing power of Christ; those who, conscious of their sins, confess them have in Christ a Saviour from whom forgiveness and cleansing from every sinful act may be freely received – not because He is indulgent and easy-going but because He is 'faithful and righteous'. He is *faithful* in that His promise is sure: those who put their trust in Him will not be let down; those who come to Him will not be cast out. The relevance in this connexion of His being *righteous* appears clearly in 2. 1, where His righteousness is associated with His advocacy. We need not press too fine a distinction between 'unrighteousness' and 'sin'; 'all unrighteousness is sin' (5. 17).

V. 10 **If we say that we have not sinned, we make him a liar, and his word is not in us.**

The third false claim is similar to the second but not identical with it. To assert that one has never sinned is to contradict the consistent witness of divine revelation and human experience. God makes provision for men as sinners; the acknowledgement of honest men confronted with the holiness of God takes the form, 'I have sinned'. 'He who does not believe God has made him a liar' (5. 10), whether the divine testimony to which he refuses credence concerns his own sin or the provision of life eternal in Christ. There is perhaps a slight difference between 'his word is not in us' at the end of verse 10 and 'the truth is not in us' at the end of verse 8; if John is moving to a climax, the situation described here is even more serious than that described in verse 8, but in the light of John 17. 17, 'thy word is truth', the distinction must be a fine one. In John 5. 38 Jesus says to His hearers in reference to the Father's witness, 'you do not have his word abiding in you, for you do not believe him whom he has sent'; again, in John 8. 37 He charges His opponents with seeking to kill Him 'because my word finds no place in you'. Such expressions in the Gospel indicate how the analogous language of the Epistle is to be understood.

NOTES

1. See A. Ehrhardt, *The Beginning* (Manchester, 1968), pp. 193 f.; he thinks it was pre-eminently Mic. 5. 2, LXX (*ap' archēs*), that was in John's mind.
2. Cf. Polycarp, *To the Philippians* 7. 2: 'let us turn back to the word which was delivered to us from the beginning (*ex archēs*)'.

3. It has been suggested that, in addition to stressing the eyewitness testimony on which the gospel was based, these words might be calculated to refute agnostic misuse of the saying quoted in 1 Cor. 2. 9 – perhaps in a form like that occurring in the *Gospel of Thomas* (Saying 17): 'I will give you what eye never saw, what ear never heard, what hand never touched . . .' (A. Ehrhardt, *The Framework of the New Testament Stories*, Manchester, 1964, pp. 28 ff.).

4. Cf. Ignatius: 'I know and believe that he was in the flesh even after the resurrection. And when he came to Peter and his companions he said to them: "Take, handle (*psēlaphaō*) me and see that I am not a bodiless phantom" ' (*To the Smyrnaeans* 3. 1 f.).

5. See pp. 18 f.

6. As in the title of G. Goodman, *The Epistle of Eternal Life* (Pickering and Inglis, 1936). On 'eternal life' see also note on 5. 11 (p. 122).

7. Cf. C. H. Dodd, *The Johannine Epistles* (London, 1946), pp. 9 ff.

8. See p. 21, n. 1, for the relevance of the term 'apostolic' in a commentary on documents from which it is absent.

9. Cf. NEB: 'you are not in fellowship with me'.

10. The principal witnesses for 'our' are Codices Sinaiticus and Vaticanus. This textual variation between the pronouns of the first and second persons plural is one of the commonest in NT because by the first century AD there was little, if any, difference in pronunciation between them.

11. If some places in OT speak of God as dwelling in 'thick darkness' (e.g. Ex. 20. 21; 1 Kings 8. 12; Psalm 97. 2), that is because His effulgent light is so unapproachable (cf. 1 Tim. 6. 16) that it must be hidden from men behind the cloud of the *shekinah*. Cf. E. R. Goodenough, *By Light, Light* (New Haven, 1935), p. 267.

12. For the phrase 'the light of life' cf. the Qumran *Rule of the Community* 3. 6 f.: 'Through the spirit of God's true counsel atonement is made for a man's ways, even for all his iniquities, so that he may see the light of life'.

13. *Rule of the Community* 3. 13 ff. Cf. note on 1 John 4. 1 (p. 104).

14. Cf. Eph. 5. 8. See also note on 1 John 2. 8 (p. 54).

15. *Rule of the Community* 3. 20 f.

16. Cf. John 8. 12 (quoted on pp. 40 f.); 12. 46; 1 John 2. 11.

17. The words 'one with another' may mean believers with fellow-believers or believers with God. It is unnecessary to insist on the one meaning as against the other, since the one implies the other.

18. In OT to be 'cleansed' from sin is synonymous with having one's sin 'atoned for'; cf. Lev. 16. 30, with reference to the Day of Atonement: 'on this day shall atonement be made for you, to cleanse you; from all your sins you shall be clean before the LORD' (LXX has the same verb for 'cleanse', *katharizō*, as John uses here). This is relevant to the NEB rendering of Gr. *hilasmos* in 1 John 2. 2 and 4. 10 as 'remedy for the defilement (of our sins)'. A. T. Hanson draws a parallel between Ps. 130 (LXX 129) and 1 John 1. 7–2. 5; he points in particular to verse 4 of the psalm, 'with thee is forgiveness (LXX *hilasmos*)', and verse 8, 'he will redeem Israel *from all its iniquities*'. His suggestion is that Psalm 130 'was considered in the early Church to refer to Christian baptism and that John had this psalm in mind as he wrote this passage in his First Epistle' (*Studies in the Pastoral Epistles*, London, 1968, pp. 91 ff.).

19. *The Epistles of St. John* (London, 1902), pp. 34 ff.

20. W. Milligan, *The Resurrection of our Lord* (London, 1894), p. 280. A similar

view of the significance of sacrificial blood-shedding in another context is presented in W. R. Smith, *The Religion of the Semites*[2] (London, 1894), pp. 269 ff., 317 ff., 338 ff.

21. Cf. A. M. Stibbs, *The Meaning of the Word 'Blood' in Scripture* (London, 1947); L. Morris, 'The Biblical Use of the Term "Blood" ', *JTS* n.s. 3 (1952), pp. 216 ff.; *The Apostolic Preaching of the Cross* (London, 1955), pp. 108 ff.; F. J. Taylor, in *A Theological Word Book of the Bible*, ed. A. Richardson (London, 1950), pp. 33 f. (*s.v.* 'Blood'). 'The interest of the New Testament is not in the material blood of Christ, but in His shed blood as the life violently taken from Him. Like the cross, the "blood of Christ" is simply another and even more graphic phrase for the death of Christ in its soteriological significance' (J. Behm, in *TDNT* i, Grand Rapids, 1964, p. 174, *s.v.* αἷμα).

22. Cf. Heb. 9. 14; 10. 2, 22.

23. Cf. 1 John 4. 1 (pp. 103 f.).

CHAPTER II

V. 1 My little children, these things write I unto you, that ye may not sin. And if any man sin, we have an [1]Advocate with the Father, Jesus Christ the righteous: v. 2 and he is the propitiation for our sins; and not for ours only, but also for the whole world.

[1] Or, *Comforter* Or, *Helper* Gr. *Paraclete*.

John uses two different Greek words in this epistle when he addresses his readers as 'children'. That used here and six other places[1] is *teknia*, the plural of *teknion*. Jesus uses it in John 13. 33 when speaking to His disciples in the upper room; Paul uses it in a tender passage in Gal. 4. 19. The other is *paidia*, the plural of *paidion*; it is used only twice in this epistle (in verses 13 and 18 of this chapter),[2] although it is much commoner than *teknia* in the New Testament as a whole and indeed in general Greek usage. Since *teknia* retains something of its diminutive force (*teknion* being the diminutive form of *teknon*),[3] it is properly translated 'little children'; *paidia*, on the other hand, while also a diminutive in form (*paidion* being the diminutive of *pais*), had lost its diminutive force by this time, so it might well be rendered 'children' (as in John 21. 5).

While insisting, against the false teachers, that it is wrong to say either that 'we have no sin' or that 'we have not sinned', John does not wish to give his readers the idea that sin may be regarded as a normal phenomenon in the Christian life. Far from it: the main purpose of his touching the subject at all is to put them on their guard against committing sin. Sin, indeed, is so thoroughly uncharacteristic of the Christian life that a life which is marked by sin cannot be called Christian; this is a point to which John returns in chapter 3. But instead of making false claims about sinlessness, a Christian should be grateful to know that, if he does

commit sin, his case is not hopeless. In the presence of God he has
an Advocate, a powerful counsel for the defence. This Advocate
does not need to resort to questionable devices to secure acquittal
for his clients; he is a *righteous* Advocate. The designation 'The
Righteous One' was used of the coming Messiah or Son of Man in
pre-Christian times,[4] and in the New Testament it appears as a
title of Jesus (cf. Acts 3. 14; 7. 52; 22. 14); but here the epithet (Gr.
dikaios) has special reference to His advocacy on His people's behalf.

In the New Testament the word 'Advocate' (Gr. *paraklētos*) is
found only five times, all in the Johannine writings; its four other
occurrences are in the Gospel, on the lips of Jesus, in reference to
the Holy Spirit as 'another Advocate' – or, as RSV has it, 'another
Counsellor' (John 14. 16; cf. 14. 26; 15. 26; 16. 7).[5] The implication of the expression 'another Advocate' is that Jesus Himself is
the primary Advocate. While the word itself does not appear outside the Johannine writings, the idea which it conveys is embedded
in primitive Christian teaching. Paul speaks of the Spirit as one who
'intercedes for the saints' (Rom. 8. 26, 27) and describes Jesus as
the one 'who is at the right hand of God, who indeed intercedes
for us' (Rom. 8. 34). The promise of Luke 12. 8, 'every one who
acknowledges me before men, the Son of Man also will acknowledge before the angels of God', found an early fulfilment in
Stephen who, having witnessed a good confession before men,
saw 'the Son of Man standing at the right hand of God' (Acts
7. 56) – in the posture of an advocate. In the Epistle to the
Hebrews, too, advocacy forms part of our Lord's intercessory
ministry as His people's high priest.[6]

This intercessory ministry is not a new activity on His part;
we recall His promise to pray for Peter that his faith might not fail
(Luke 22. 32) and in the upper room His high-priestly prayer, as it
has been aptly called from the time of David Chytraeus in the
sixteenth century, embraces in its intercession both His immediate
disciples (John 17. 9–19) and their converts (John 17. 20 ff.). But
now this ministry is reinforced by His perfect sacrifice.

There is no question of this Advocate's having to extort a
favourable verdict from a reluctant Judge; His presence before the

Father is advocacy enough by itself, for He is there as the 'propitiation' for His people's sins. With the word *hilasmos* (used in the
New Testament only here and in 1 John 4. 10) we may compare
hilastērion (from the same root) in Rom. 3. 25. We need not stay to
enquire whether 'expiation' (RSV) or 'remedy for defilement' (NEB)[7]
would be a preferable rendering of *hilasmos*; 'propitiation' or
'atonement' will do well enough, if we use either word in its
biblical sense – not as something which men must do to placate
God,[8] but something which God has provided in His grace to
bring men into His presence with the assurance that they are
accepted by Him, since He has removed the barrier that kept them
at a distance – guilt, with its attendant retribution, the 'punishment' which is banished by 'perfect love' (4. 18). 'Now in Christ
Jesus', says another New Testament letter, 'you who once were far
off have been brought near in the blood of Christ' (Eph. 2. 13);
this is the truth that John states here in different language.[9] Nor
will John let his readers think of their blessings in restrictive terms.
The propitiation that has availed to wipe out their sins is sufficient
to do the same for all. Jesus is 'the general Saviour of mankind' as
well as the particular Saviour of each believer. According to the
Fourth Gospel, He is 'the true light that enlightens every man'
(John 1. 9) or, in the forerunner's language, He is 'the Lamb of God,
who takes away the sin of the world' (John 1. 29).[10] Christians must
not rest content with the assurance of their own salvation, but spread
the joyful news world-wide. I know of no commentary on 1 John
2. 2 so apposite as Charles Wesley's hymn, 'Arise, my soul, arise':[11]

> He ever lives above
>   For me to intercede,
> His all-redeeming love,
>   His precious blood, to plead;
> His blood atoned for all our race,
> And sprinkles now the throne of grace.
>
> Five bleeding wounds He bears,
>   Received on Calvary;
> They pour effectual prayers,
>   They strongly speak for me;
> Forgive him, O forgive! they cry,
> Nor let that ransom'd sinner die!

3 THE NEW COMMANDMENT (2. 3–17)

(a) *The test of obedience* (2. 3–6)

V. 3 And hereby know we that we know him, if we keep his commandments.

The test of obedience is simple and can be applied to all kinds of religious profession. 'If you love me', says Jesus to His disciples in the upper room, 'you will keep my commandments' (John 14. 15). In our present passage the object 'him' probably denotes God, since the seceding teachers had so much to say about their know-ledge of God, but since the knowledge of God is mediated through Christ, to know the Father is to know the Son. Those who boasted of their knowledge of God could give proof of their claim by their obedience to Him. The expression 'hereby we know' or something very similar occurs frequently in this epistle when a practical test of verbal profession is laid down (see 2. 5b; 3. 10, 16, 19, 24b; 4. 2, 13; 5. 2).

V. 4 He that saith, I know him, and keepeth not his commandments, is a liar, and the truth is not in him:

This sentence is the converse of the preceding one. The same damning indictment is pronounced against one who falsely claims to know God as is pronounced in 1. 8 against those who say they have no sin. Here we have the first of three statements introduced by 'he that saith', where the introductory words serve much the same purpose as 'if we say' in 1. 6, 8, 10; the two others come in verses 6 and 9 of this chapter. They all underline the importance of matching profession with practice.

V. 5a but whoso keepeth his word, in him verily hath the love of God been perfected.

'The love of God' here is 'our love for God' (in other words, 'of God' represents the objective genitive); as our *knowledge* of God is to be tested by our obedience, so too is our *love* for Him – in fact, obedience is the full flowering of our love for Him. 'This is the love of God, that we keep his commandments' (1 John 5. 3). What is involved in this perfection of love is spelt out in greater detail in 1 John 4. 12, 17 ff.; there too it is made plain that the love of believers for God (and for one another) is the response to His love for them.

V. 5b Hereby know we that we are in him: v. 6 he that saith he abideth in him ought himself also to walk even as he walked.

A further test is introduced, as in verse 3, by the words 'hereby know we'. It is easy for a man to claim that he is 'in God' – that his life is bound up in the life of God, that he has fellowship with God. (To distinguish between being in the Father and being in the Son is to make a distinction without a difference; the one involves the other.) But such a claim – introduced, as in verse 4, by 'he that saith' – is to be verified by a searching practical test. As we have been told already that no one who walks in darkness can have fellowship with the God of light, so now it is emphasized that the character of God will be displayed in those who abide in Him. And the character of God is not something about which we are left to speculate. God incarnate lived on earth; the character of God has been manifested in the conduct of Christ. The emphatic pronoun *ekeinos* occurs in a personal sense six times in this letter, always with reference to Christ, and usually with reference to Christ as His people's example; indeed, in four occurrences out of the six (of which this is one) it appears in the phrase *kathōs ekeinos*, 'as *he*' (see also 3. 3, 7; 4. 17).[12] We know how Christ conducted Himself; the glory which His disciples discerned in Him was 'full of grace and truth', and something of these qualities will be evident in anyone who truly 'abides'[13] in Him, which is another way of denoting the experience of truly 'knowing' Him (verse 4). What is meant by abiding in Him is illustrated at greater length in the parable of the vine and the branches in John 15. 1–17; as it is the life of the vine in the branches that enables them to produce the fruit of the vine, so the life of Christ in His people will be manifested as their behaviour resembles His.

(b) The test of love (2. 7–11)

V. 7 Beloved, no new commandment write I unto you, but an old commandment which ye had from the beginning: the old commandment is the word which ye heard.

Love and obedience are inextricably interwoven because all the commandments of God are summed up in the law of love. 'You shall love the Lord your God' was the authoritative summary of the Old Testament law (Deut. 6. 5), and when Jesus was asked which was the greatest commandment of all, this was the one which He quoted, coupling with it the similar commandment of Lev. 19. 18 enjoining love to one's neighbour (Mark 12. 28 ff.). These words of Jesus were embedded from the earliest days in the apostles' witness: 'the whole law', says Paul, 'is fulfilled in one word, "You shall love your neighbour as yourself" ' (Gal. 5. 14; cf. Rom. 13. 8–10). So John, in underlining afresh the law of love, is not telling his readers anything they did not already know; it is no innovation but 'an old commandment' which they had been taught 'from the beginning' – an expression which, as in the opening clause of the epistle, denotes the beginning of the gospel. The apostolic witness which they received at the commencement of their Christian experience included both the record of God's saving work in Christ and instruction (based on the teaching of Christ Himself) about the way of life befitting the beneficiaries of this saving work. In this 'word' which they 'heard' in those early days the commandment of love had a foremost place; in this sense it was an 'old commandment'.

V. 8 Again, a new commandment write I unto you, which thing is true in him and in you; because the darkness is passing away, and the true light already shineth.

Yet, old as the commandment of love is in one sense, there is a sense in which it is new. Jesus had summed it up in words from the Old Testament law which were centuries old by His time, but when He laid it on His disciples afresh in the upper room, He called it 'a new commandment': 'A new commandment I give to you, that you love one another' (John 13. 34a). And it was new because by His own fulfilment of it He was giving it a depth of meaning which it had not possessed before: ' . . . even as I have loved you, that you also love one another. By this all men will know that you are my disciples, if you have love for one another' (John 13. 34b, 35). This aspect of the 'new commandment' will be insisted upon repeatedly in this epistle, and indeed it is implied here, where John tells his readers that the substance of this commandment has come 'true [perfectly] in him [i.e. in Christ] and [in measure] in you'. But here it is 'a new commandment' because it is the characteristic commandment of the new age. Christ, the Light of the world, came to dispel the darkness of sin and ignorance and to inaugurate the era of light and love. The language is not peculiar to the Johannine writings in the New Testament. In 1 Thess. 5. 5, for example, Paul says, 'you are all sons of the light and sons of the day; we are not of the night or of darkness'; in Col. 1. 12 f. God has qualified His people 'to share in the inheritance of the saints in light' and has delivered them 'from the dominion of darkness', while in Eph. 5. 8 believers in Christ are told: 'once you were darkness, but now you are light in the Lord'. But the terminology of light and darkness is specially characteristic of John,[14] and he uses it to describe the difference that Christ has made. Jewish eschatology distinguished 'this age' from 'that age', i.e. the resurrection age (cf. Luke 20. 34 f.), sometimes interposing 'the days of the Messiah' between the two. This general framework is adopted by the New Testament writers, but it is radically modified and re-interpreted in terms of the work of Christ. In His ministry the new age ('the kingdom of God') is in process of inauguration; when His ministry is crowned by His death and resurrection, it is fully inaugurated (the kingdom of God has 'come with power'). The 'days of the Messiah' have begun with His exaltation to the throne of God, from which He reigns until God has put all His enemies beneath His feet (1 Cor. 15. 25). For His people the new age has been anticipated; having died with Him they share His resurrection life and are already enthroned with Him in the heavenly realm, in the sense of Eph. 2. 6. Eternal life ('the life of the age to come') is theirs to possess and enjoy here and now. All this is made possible for them by the Spirit, who both makes effective in them what Christ did for them and enables them to realize the heritage of glory which will be theirs in fulness at the consummation. But as long as the new age is inaugurated but not yet consummated (as it will be by the *parousia* of Christ), the old age is still in being. Believers who belong spiritually to 'that age' live temporally in 'this age'. Although 'the true light' is already shining, the darkness has not passed completely away; it is in process of 'passing away'.[15] Thanks to the victory of Christ, the outcome of the conflict between light and darkness is a foregone conclusion, but the conflict is still going on. Hence the tension of Christian life in the present world, a tension reflected throughout this epistle, not to say throughout the whole New Testament. In the words of Lord Eustace Percy:

> Ever since Christianity was first preached the Christian citizen has been a puzzle both to himself and to his rulers. By the elementary necessities of his creed he has been a man living in two worlds. In one he has been a member of a national community, in the other of a community 'taken out of the nations'. In one he has been bound to obey and enforce the laws of his State, in the other to measure his conduct by standards not recognised by those laws and often inconsistent with them. This dualism has been made tolerable only by the prospect of a reconciliation. That prospect is, again, an elementary necessity of the Christian creed. Somehow, somewhere, the conflict of loyalties will end. The kingdom of this world will pass: the Kingdom of God will be established.[16]

V. 9 He that saith he is in the light, and hateth his brother, is in the darkness even until now. v. 10 He that loveth his brother abideth in the light, and there is none occasion of stumbling in him. v. 11 But he that hateth his brother is in the darkness, and walketh in the darkness, and knoweth not whither he goeth, because the darkness hath blinded his eyes.

Since the new commandment of love is the distinctive commandment of the new age, the test of obedience is pre-eminently a test of love. The claim to be 'in the light' – once more introduced by the phrase 'he that saith' – is a claim to have fellowship with God. In 1. 6 John has insisted that such a claim is incompatible with walking in darkness; here he insists that such a claim is incompatible with loveless behaviour. No one is allowed to imagine that he can get away with a claim to be a lover of God on the ground that this is an inward attitude, invisible to other men. The twin commandments of love to God and love to one's neighbour are like two sides of a coin; the one is essential to the other. So the claim to live 'in the light', to enjoy fellowship with the God of light, must be tested by a man's treatment of his brother. The word 'treatment' should be emphasized because, as John makes clear later, it is not a matter of sentimental feelings and language, familiar in certain brands of pietism, but of loving 'in deed and in truth' (3. 18).

That the rights of knowledge must be exercised in consistency with the claims of love is emphasized in other parts of the New Testament as well as in the Johannine writings, as Paul's teaching about the obligations due to fellow-believers with weaker consciences illustrates (cf. Rom. 14. 15; 1 Cor. 8. 11). Paul, indeed, insists that knowledge divorced from love is not true knowledge; 'but if one loves God, one is known by him' (1 Cor. 8. 3) and his knowledge of God will manifest itself in his love towards others. The two great affirmations about God in John's first epistle are that 'God is light' (1. 5) and 'God is love' (4. 8, 16); the knowledge of God will therefore produce holiness resembling His and acts of love resembling His.

John characteristically sees life in terms of black and white; intermediate greys have no existence for him. So there is no middle course between love and hatred, and by hatred he does not necessarily mean positive animosity but mere lack of love. Lack of love (including that form of it which postpones an act of charity to a more convenient season) can blind a man's spiritual vision as effectively as the prejudice arising from hatred does, so that he is

tripped up by all kinds of moral obstacles that lie in life's way, and
is disabled from forming ethical decisions which are crystal-clear
to his brother whose love of heart and hand maintains him in fellowship with God, in whose light he sees light.[17] If it is possible, on the
one hand, to over-simplify moral issues through one-sided prejudice or inadequate appreciation of the relevant facts, it is possible, on the other hand, to find them more complex than they really
are through failure to assess them in the light of the love of God.
This consideration applies not only to personal ethics but to issues
of global scale.

John has more to say about divine love later in this epistle;[18]
here he is content to anticipate his fuller exposition of the subject
by insisting that religious profession must be tested by the presence
or absence of love in action. Before he proceeds to a further stage
of his argument, he rounds off his statement of the 'new commandment' with two paragraphs of encouragement and warning.

(c) Encouragement to three age-groups (2. 12–14)

**V. 12   I write unto you, *my* little children, because your
sins are forgiven you for his name's sake.**

**V. 13a   I write unto you, fathers, because ye know him
which is from the beginning.**

**V. 13b   I write unto you, young men, because ye have over-
come the evil one.**

**V. 13c   [1]I have written unto you, little children, because ye
know the Father.**

**V. 14a   [1]I have written unto you, fathers, because ye know
him which is from the beginning.**

**V. 14b   [1]I have written unto you, young men, because ye
are strong, and the word of God abideth in you, and ye have
overcome the evil one.**

[1] Or, *I wrote.*

No completely satisfying explanation has been given by commentators of the duplication of this threefold encouragement. The

three sentences in verses 13c and 14a, b may represent a later and fuller re-writing of what is preserved as an earlier draft in verses 12 and 13a, b. The tense of the verb 'write' changes from the first to the second draft; in the former it is the present *graphō*, in the latter it is the aorist, *egrapsa*, but there is no material significance in the change, since the aorist 'I have written' is here probably the epistolary aorist, denoting the time-perspective of the readers rather than of the writer. Another minor distinction is that between '*my* little children' (*teknia*) in verse 12 and 'little children' (*paidia*) in verse 13c; as both nouns take their precise meanings from their correlation in the two contexts with 'fathers' and 'young men', they must be synonymous, indicating a more restricted group than the general 'my little children' (*teknia*) of verses 1 and 28 or 'little children' (*paidia*) of verse 18.

The threefold grouping relates to spiritual maturity, not years reckoned by the calendar. Even if, in the third Christian generation, there was a growing tendency for spiritual maturity and natural age to coincide (as we may find in many Christian churches today when we compare the elderhood with the Bible class), nevertheless it is spiritual experience that is emphasized. The younger believers have made a beginning by knowing their sins forgiven for Christ's sake. They have also started to appreciate their new status as children of God (cf. 3. 1) in that they have come to 'know the Father'. The senior believers, as is stated twice, have come to 'know him who is from the beginning'. This is the same God as the children have come to know, but whereas the children have come to recognize Him as their Father – demonstrating thereby, as Paul would say, that they have received the Spirit that makes them sons,[20] the Spirit of Christ Himself, since like Him they now call God 'Abba, Father!' (Rom. 8. 15 f.; Gal. 4. 6) – the fathers, through long experience of Him, have come to know Him in a fuller and deeper fashion. While it is to be hoped that all the children of God know Him as their Father and love spontaneously to address Him and speak of Him thus, there are some men and women whom we naturally describe as people who 'know God' because over the years they have sought, and been freely granted, such access to the heart of God that God knows them, as He knew Moses, 'face to face' (Deut. 34. 10).[21]

The *children*, then, have made a good beginning by knowing that through Christ their sins have been forgiven and that God is their Father, and with proper guidance and care they may advance from there; the fathers have attained a ripe and intimate acquaintance with the eternal God (whatever 'from the beginning'[22] may mean elsewhere in these epistles, it can denote nothing less than God's eternity here); but it is the *young men* who receive chief attention – as is indicated perhaps even by their being placed last in each of the two drafts. They are the believers who have reached a stage of spiritual development where they are expected to bear the burden and heat of the day; they are the church's first line of defence against attack, whether that attack takes the form of overt persecution or of subtle undermining of Christian faith and life. The young men whom John addresses have shown themselves worthy of his commendation; they 'have overcome the evil one', as he assures them twice, and thus they have proved that they 'are strong', endued with spiritual power, and that 'the word of God abides' in them. In all the main Johannine writings – Gospel,[23] First Epistle[24] and Revelation[25] alike – the theme of overcoming is present, and in all it is through Christ, the supreme Overcomer, that His people overcome. When in the wilderness He overcame 'the evil one',[26] it was by virtue of the word of God abiding in Him ('It is written', 'It is said', was His weapon); so His people, according to Paul, may not only 'quench all the flaming darts of the evil one' by means of 'the shield of faith', but may go over to the offensive against their spiritual foe with 'the sword of the Spirit, which is the word of God' (Eph. 6. 16 f.). (While *rhēma* is the noun rendered 'word' in Eph. 6. 17 and not *logos*, as in our present passage,[27] the point is that, for both Christ and Christians, 'the word He hath spoken shall surely prevail'.)

(d) Warning against the world (2. 15–17)

V. 15   Love not the world, neither the things that are in the world. If any man love the world, the love of the Father is not

in him. v. 16 For all that is in the world, the lust of the flesh, and the lust of the eyes, and the vainglory of life, is not of the Father, but is of the world. v. 17 And the world passeth away, and the lust thereof: but he that doeth the will of God abideth for ever.

The 'world' (Gr. *kosmos*) has a wide range of meaning in the Johannine writings, and the context must determine, from one place to another, which phase of its meaning is to be understood. On the one hand, the world was made by God through the agency of His 'Word' (John 1. 10); it was loved by God (John 3. 16); it is the object of God's saving purpose (John 3. 17). Christ is the Light of the world (John 1. 9; 8. 12; 9. 5), the Saviour of the world (John 4. 42; 1 John 4. 14), the propitiation for the whole world (1 John 2. 2), 'the Lamb of God, who takes away the sin of the world' (John 1. 29). On the other hand, the world at present lies in the grip of 'the evil one' (1 John 5. 19) and is therefore orientated against God;[28] accordingly, when He who is the Word and the Light came into the world, the world failed to recognize Him (John 1. 10; 1 John 3. 1) and similarly it does not recognize His followers (1 John 3. 1); indeed, it hates them (John 15. 18 f.; 17. 14; 1 John 3. 13), just as it hated Him (John 7. 7; 15. 18, 23, 24, 25). What John says about the world is similar to what Paul, in different language, says about the creation: it 'was subjected to futility, not of its own will but by the will of him who subjected it in hope; because the creation itself will be set free from its bondage to decay and obtain the glorious liberty of the children of God' (Rom. 8. 21).

What John warns his readers against in the present passage is the world orientated against God, 'the godless world', as the NEB paraphrases it. The spirit that dominates the world so orientated, 'the spirit that is now at work in the sons of disobedience', as it is put in Eph. 2. 2, is inimical to the love of God and to the uninhibited outflowing of His love in the lives of His people. Conformity to that spirit is wordliness. Worldliness, it must be emphasized in face of much superficial thought and language on the subject, does not lie in things we do or in places we frequent; it lies in the human heart, in the set of human affections and attitudes. It may manifest itself in petty but soul-stunting ambitions like 'keeping up with the Joneses'; it may manifest itself in unthinking acquiescence in current policies of monstrous malignity, as when too many Christians in Nazi Germany found it possible to go along with (or close their eyes to) their government's genocidal treatment of the Jews. Worldliness of the latter sort is not that which has usually been denounced by popular pietism; our Saviour's remark about the gnat and the camel may come to mind in this connection. If, in a world where the richer nations tend to become richer and the poorer to become poorer, the administration of a richer nation makes further increases in economic prosperity a major plank in its platform, the Christian – especially, perhaps, the Christian who prefers to remain as detached as possible from political responsibility – must be constantly vigilant lest his own life reflect the unadmitted assumptions underlying such a policy. To share political, social or economic presuppositions which are inconsistent with the Father's love is one form of worldliness.

Indeed, John's understanding of worldliness seems to be very much of this character, when we consider the three elements which he specifies as making up what is 'in the world'.[29] For the 'desire of the flesh' and the 'desire of the eyes'[30] and the 'pretentiousness of life', as it may be rendered,[31] comprise the outlook which is commonly designated materialism. Worldliness does not reside in 'things', but it does certainly reside in our concentration on 'things'. If our affections, instead of being set on what is of permanent importance, are set on passing things that the heart desires and the eye delights in, or things that encourage us to have a good conceit of ourselves, we are fearfully impoverished. If my reputation, my 'public image', matters more to me than the glory of God or the well-being of my fellows, the 'pretentiousness of life' has become the object of my idol-worship.

This 'pretentiousness of life' is equated in the lexicon of Bauer–Arndt–Gingrich with 'pride in one's possessions', and it can be a very subtle enemy of the soul. My house, my garden, my car, my library or some other 'status symbol' – whatever it is I take most pride in – can minister to this peril. One begins to understand why R. C. Chapman, returning to live in the town where he used to drive his carriage and pair, with coachman and footman, took a working-class house in a back street: 'my pride never got over it', he said.[32] But even such an action as that, on the part of a lesser soul than Chapman, might simply be an inverted form of 'the pretentiousness of life' – the exceptionally deadly 'pride that apes humility'. The one effective antidote to worldliness is to have one's heart so filled with the Father's love that it has no room for any love that is incompatible with that.

Another form of worldliness, highly relevant to the situation in which John wrote, is the adaptation of the gospel to some contemporary tendency or philosophy or spirit of the age. It used to be said by acute foreign observers that Christians in this country had difficulty in distinguishing the interests of the kingdom of God from those of the British Empire; nowadays this tendency to confuse the gospel with national or imperial ideals may be more clearly manifested in equal and opposite degree in other parts of the world. There are other Christians, more internationally minded, who are prone to identify the rule of God in the world with the advancement of the United Nations. Deplorable as these forms of worldliness are, they are not so deplorable as the identification of the kingdom of God with this or that ecclesiastical organization, whether it be the World Council of Churches or my own particular 'Little Bethel'. Such an identification has too often served as an excuse for all sorts of ethically dubious policies and actions. Nothing that is unrighteous or uncharitable in itself is ever truly done for the glory of God, however much we may persuade ourselves that it is so.

Reference has already been made to that variety of worldliness which consists in 're-stating' the gospel so thoroughly in terms of the current climate of opinion that the 're-statement' bears no relation to the original essence of the gospel.[33] John deals faithfully with proponents of such a 're-statement' in his day; the same sort of thing is perfectly familiar today. When we are told that 'thoughtful men can no longer accept' one or another of the articles of the historic Christian faith, we need not be overmuch concerned; the way in which this affirmation is made begs the question at issue. Some 'thoughtful men' find no intellectual difficulty in believing what other 'thoughtful men' reject; so much depends on the axioms or premises on which one's thought is based. We may listen respectfully to a well-reasoned case for the acceptance or repudiation of some belief or other, but if the argument amounts to no more than that the belief is in conformity (or out of conformity) with the contemporary climate of opinion, it is wise to bear in mind the possibility that the contemporary climate of opinion may be wrong.

The prevalent secularism of western man has so influenced some Christian thinkers of our own day that they endeavour to 're-state' Christian doctrine or Christian ethics in terms which would be equally relevant whether one believed in the living God or not – sometimes, indeed, in terms which would make better sense if the living God were dismissed from our thinking. Whatever such a 're-statement' may properly be called, it cannot be called Christianity. As the Docetism which John attacked was one way in which worldliness was invading the church at the end of the first century, so the passing fashion of the 'death of God' theology (a contradiction in terms if ever there was one) is one way among many in which worldliness has invaded the church today. There may be something to be said for what has been called 'holy worldliness', if that means giving that place to the material order as God's creation which the Bible gives it, instead of dismissing all things temporal as evil; but a system of thought or way of life from which the Creator is deliberately excluded is a manifestation of *unholy* worldliness.

The world, as Paul said, is to be 'used' by the Christian as a means to the true end of his Christian living, not as an end in itself, 'for the form of this world is passing away' (1 Cor. 7. 31). So, says John, 'the world is passing away'[34] and so is all our desire for it – or, if desire (Gr. *epithymia*) can be taken here in a concrete sense, all the desirable things that it contains. Why should heirs

of the eternal world concentrate their interests and ambitions on
such a transient order? Why should they place all their eggs in
such a perishable basket? Why does Christian practice so often fall
short of Christian profession? If it is indeed in the ever-living
God that we have placed our trust, if it is by His love that our lives
are dominated, then His interests will be paramount with us. His
kingdom, into which He has called His people, is the one un-
shakable order.

'Seek first his kingdom and his righteousness', said our Lord,
'and all these things [temporal necessities] shall be yours as well'
(Matt. 6. 33). It was thought by some to be mildly blasphemous
when, in recent years, an African ruler modified this wording in a
public inscription to read: 'Seek ye first the political kingdom . . .'
(and he soon discovered how mistaken he was). But without
overtly modifying our Lord's words, many people who would
regard themselves as better Christians than Dr. Nkrumah put
their own private glosses on them (to be proved as mistaken in their
turn as he was). Since all live *to* God (Luke 20. 38) it is well if all
live *for* Him: 'he who does the will of God abides for ever'.

4   THE TEACHING OF ANTICHRIST (2. 18–27)

(a) Many antichrists (2. 18)

V. 18   **Little children, it is the last hour: and as ye heard
that antichrist cometh, even now have there arisen many
antichrists; whereby we know that it is the last hour.**

Here John addresses all his readers as his 'children' (*paidia*).[35]
The days between the first appearance of Christ and His
coming advent in glory are the 'last days' in New Testament parlance – the days which witness the fulfilment of all that the Old
Testament prophets foretold as destined to happen 'in the latter
days'. The 'last hour' (*eschatē hōra*) might be regarded as an
alternative expression for the 'last days', but more probably it
denotes the terminal phase of the 'last days', like the 'last time'
(*kairos eschatos*) of 1 Pet. 1. 5 at which the final salvation is to be

revealed. According to Jude 18 the apostles of Christ foretold that scoffers would arise 'in the last time' (*ep' eschatou chronou*); Jude sees the fulfilment of their words in the emergence of the false teachers whom he denounces in his epistle. So John infers from the appearance of the false teachers against whom he warns his readers that the end-time Antichrist is now at hand and that his spirit is active in these teachers; that is how 'we know that it is the last hour'.

But in what sense was it 'the last hour'? John may have thought that in fact the last decade of the first century was five minutes to midnight on the clock of destiny: that he and his fellow-Christians were witnessing the onset of the great revolt which would immediately precede the *parousia*. Nothing that he knew precluded such an expectation; much that he knew encouraged it. But if 'the last hour' be understood thus in terms of common chronology, what validity could John's expectation and language have for his readers today, between eighteen and nineteen centuries later? If the last hour is to be dated between AD 90 and 100, what terminology can be applied to AD 1970? The truth is, as John Henry Newman put it last century, that:

> though time intervene between Christ's first and second coming, it is not *recognized* (as I may say) in the Gospel scheme, but is, as it were, an accident. For so it was, that up to Christ's coming in the flesh, the course of things ran straight towards that end, nearing it by every step; but now, under the Gospel, that course has (if I may so speak) altered its direction, as regards His second coming, and runs, not towards the end, but along it, and on the brink of it; and is at all times near that great event, which, did it run towards it, it would at once run into. Christ, then, is ever at our doors.[36]

In the Christian era it is always five minutes to midnight. But as 'the course of things' runs along the edge of the final consummation, that edge at times becomes a knife-edge, and at such times the sense of its being 'the last hour' is specially acute.

So it was with John. That Antichrist would come he and his readers knew, and in the false teachers he discerned the agents, or at least the forerunners, of Antichrist, sharing his nature so completely that they could be called 'many antichrists.' 'You have heard', he says, 'that Antichrist is coming'. But this is the first occasion in the New Testament – or indeed in the Greek Bible – where this term appears. John is the only biblical writer who uses it; he does so in this present context (verses 18, 22), in 1 John 4. 3 and in 2 John 7. It must not be inferred that his readers had heard something unknown to readers of the earlier New Testament letters or to those who listened to our Lord's teaching; the word 'Antichrist' may be peculiar to John's letters in biblical literature, but the idea expressed by the word is not.

If we ask where and when John's readers had heard of the coming of Antichrist, the answer probably is that they heard of it from their first instructors in the faith, but these instructors did not invent the doctrine; they delivered what they themselves had first received. One of the earlier New Testament letters includes a passage that is specially relevant in this regard: the passage is 2 Thess. 2. 1–12, where Paul warns his Thessalonian converts against unsettling forms of eschatological expectation which lack any foundation. The day of the Lord, he says, is not here yet –

> for that day will not come, unless the rebellion comes first, and the man of lawlessness is revealed, the son of perdition, who opposes and exalts himself against every so-called god or object of worship, so that he takes his seat in the temple of God, proclaiming himself to be God. Do you not remember that when I was still with you I told you this? And now[37] you know what is restraining him so that he may be revealed in his time. For the mystery of lawlessness is already at work; only he who now restrains it will do so until he is out of the way. And then the lawless one will be revealed, and the Lord Jesus will slay him with the breath of his mouth and destroy him by his appearing and his coming. The coming of the lawless one by the activity of Satan will be with all power and with pretended signs and wonders, and with all wicked deception for those who are to perish, because they refused to love the truth and so be saved.[38]

John's readers had no doubt received teaching to much the same effect as Paul gave to the Thessalonian Christians both while he was still with them and in the words just quoted from 2 Thessalonians. That is to say, a day would come when the restraint at present imposed on the forces of lawlessness and anarchy by the power of law and order would be removed, and lawlessness would break forth in all its malignity, incarnated in a sinister figure called 'the man of lawlessness' or 'the lawless one'. This 'lawless one' is appointed to final destruction by the brightness of the epiphany of the true Christ. But during the heyday of his reign he would claim divine honours, and so skilfully would he hoodwink men by impressive signs, performed by Satan's aid, that they would bow to his claims and follow him blindly to perdition. It is to this figure that John probably refers when he says, 'You have heard that Antichrist is coming'.

But even Paul was not the first to give such teaching, although he gave it to the Thessalonians, both by word of mouth and in writing, as early as AD 50. His description of 'the lawless one' setting himself up as God in the very temple of God recalls our Lord's words about 'the abomination of desolation standing where he ought not'[39] (Mark 13. 14, RV) – the reference being apparently to a person who embodies the principle of idolatrous outrage portrayed in similar terms in the book of Daniel.[40]

To the New Testament picture of Antichrist several historical figures and events have contributed: Antiochus Epiphanes banning the worship of Israel's God and turning the Jerusalem temple over to the cult of Olympian Zeus, of whom he himself claimed to be the manifestation on earth (167 BC);[41] the Emperor Gaius demanding that his image be set up in the temple at Jerusalem to show his Jewish subjects that they must offer sacrifice *to* him as well as *for* him (AD 40);[42] the Roman soldiers setting up their legionary standards in the temple court, opposite the east gate, and sacrificing to them in celebration of their victory (AD 70).[43] In the eyes of pious Jews these persons or incidents were blasphemous, inspired by a spirit hostile to God, variously called Belial (*Beliar* in Greek)[44] or Mastema[45] (we may compare the role of Satan in 2 Thess. 2. 9 or of the dragon in Rev. 13. 2, 4). But while they made their contribution to the New Testament picture of Antichrist, the New Testament picture is controlled by the fact that God has revealed Himself definitively and brought His salvation near in Jesus, His Son, the long-expected Christ; in the mind of the church, Antichrist is so called because he claims for himself the honour that rightly belongs to Christ. The imperial beast of Rev. 13 is Anti-christ (in fact, although it is not expressly so called in Revelation) not simply because of its persecution of the church but because it claims universal worship. When Christians were commanded to acknowledge Caesar as Lord in the sense which was reserved for Christ alone, they recognized Caesar as Antichrist and refused his demand. In the same way their successors of more recent times have recognized and resisted the spirit of Antichrist in modern totalitarian systems which have endeavoured to enslave the souls of men.

But the early Christians recognized Antichrist not only in the enemy who attacked them from without but also in the enemy who seduced them from within. In this sense *antichristos* is practically synonymous with *pseudochristos*, the word used in Mark 13. 22 where our Lord warns His disciples that '*false Christs* and false prophets will arise and show signs and wonders, to lead astray, if possible, the elect'. It is people of this latter class – 'deceivers', as he calls them in 2 John 7 (where the noun *planos* is related to the verb *apo–planaō* rendered 'lead astray' in Mark 13. 22) – that John has in mind when he warns his readers that 'many antichrists' have already appeared. He is not the only New Testament writer to think in this way of subverters of the apostolic teaching. Jude, for example, describes other false teachers as 'loudmouthed boasters', echoing the language used in Dan. 7. 8 of the 'little horn' with 'a mouth speaking great things' and in Dan. 11. 36 of the 'wilful king' who will 'speak astonishing things against the God of gods' (the Theodotionic Greek version of Daniel[46] uses the same adjective, *hyperonka*, in the latter passage as is used in Jude 16 and 2 Peter 2. 18, where RV renders 'great swelling words'). The little horn and the wilful king of Daniel, two figures which were identical from the start, are regularly interpreted of Antichrist in early Christian literature.[47]

(b) The test of perseverance (2. 19)

V. 19   **They went out from us, but they were not of us; for if they had been of us, they would have continued with us:**

but *they went out*, **that they might be made manifest ¹how that they all are not of us.**

¹ Or, *that not all are of us.*

To the tests already laid down – the test of obedience and the test of love – another, the test of perseverance or continuance, is now introduced. Steadfast persistence in the way of God, without turning aside from it, is inculcated and commended throughout the biblical record. As the parable of the sower teaches, to make a spectacular beginning is not the important thing; it is those who 'hear the word and accept it and bear fruit' (Mark 4. 20), not those who merely 'endure for a while' (Mark 4. 17), who show the genuineness of their profession. The perseverance of the saints is a biblical doctrine,⁴⁸ but it is not a doctrine designed to lull the indifferent into a sense of false security; it means that perseverance is an essential token of sanctity. Not that perseverance is the product of the saints' native resolution and energy; it is He who 'began a good work' in them who 'will bring it to completion at the day of Jesus Christ' (Phil. 1. 6). But the maintenance and completion of the good work provide the evidence that the good work was ever begun. When Paul, not without reason, says to the Corinthian church, 'Do you not realize that Jesus Christ is in you? – unless indeed you fail to meet the test!' (2 Cor. 13. 5), he implies that all those in whom the risen Christ is present by His Spirit will indeed meet the test, while those who fail to meet the test, who show themselves 'reprobate' (*adokimoi*), prove by that fact that the root of the matter was never in them, whatever appearance of genuineness they may once have presented. Continuance is the test of reality.

So in the present situation the fact that the dissenters had left the apostolic fellowship simply showed that at heart they had never belonged to it. Had they been securely built on the foundation of eternal life, they would not have been so easily shifted from it. John's words are not applicable (although they have sometimes been misapplied) to people who leave one Christian company for another; they are applicable only to people who deliberately abandon the ground of Christianity rightly so called – and one should be quite certain that this is what they have done before speaking or thinking of them in these terms. John, however, is concerned that his readers should not be shaken in their faith by the secession of their former associates. The situation was not one in which a group of true believers held a position at variance with that held by another group of true believers; the seceding group by their action had shown that they were not true believers at all.

The last clause of verse 19, introduced by the distinctive Johannine expression *all' hina* ('but . . . that'),[49] is ambiguous. The two senses which it can bear are indicated in the text and footnote respectively of the NEB. 'They went out', says the NEB text, 'so that it might be clear that not all in our company truly belong to it'. But the variant rendering in the footnote runs: 'so that it might be clear that none of them truly belong to us'. The footnote rendering does little more than repeat what has just been said in the first part of the verse; the rendering in the text, which is probably to be preferred, discloses the general truth involved in a special situation. Membership in a Christian society does not always imply that one belongs to the persevering saints; enrolment in the register of a local church on earth does not necessarily carry with it enrolment in the heavenly book of life.

(c) Distinguishing truth and error (2.20–27)

V. 20   And ye have an anointing from the Holy One, [1]and ye know all things. v. 21 I have not written unto you because ye know not the truth, but because ye know it, and [2]because no lie is of the truth.

> [1] Some very ancient authorities read *and ye all know.*
> [2] Or, *that.*

The seceders claimed to have been initiated into an advanced grade of knowledge, and may have spoken disparagingly of those who remained content with 'elementary' teaching like those whom they left behind. C. S. Lewis has warned us of the seductiveness of 'the inner ring',[50] the temptation to gain admission at all costs to that exclusive élite of the people who really matter, who know what's what. The fascination of such an inner circle can be as powerful and dangerous in religion as in society. We are flattered by the idea that we are different from the rank and file, that we have access to deeper teaching, to more esoteric truth, even, it may be (and this is supremely soul-destroying), to a higher level of holiness than the majority. Our Lord crushed such pretensions when He thanked God for hiding from the wise and understanding things which were revealed to babes (Matt. 11. 25). Paul did the same when he told the Corinthian Christians who prided themselves on their intellectual attainments that he could impart the 'secret and hidden wisdom of God' only to those who were spiritually mature – that is, mature in *agapē* rather than in *gnōsis* – and to all of those (1 Cor. 2. 6–3. 3); or when he emphasized to the Colossians (who were being invited in their day to savour the attractions of a superior brand of wisdom) that his commission consisted in 'warning *every man* and teaching *every man* in all wisdom, that we may present *every man* mature in Christ' (Col. 1. 28). So John assures his readers at a later date that the 'anointing' they have received 'from the Holy One' admits them to the true knowledge. Paul had used the same term in relation to the gift of the Spirit: 'it is God', he writes to the Corinthians (coupling them with himself and his colleagues), 'who . . . has anointed us;[51] he has put his seal upon us and given us his Spirit in our hearts as a guarantee' (2. Cor. 1. 21, 22). Of these three terms by which the bestowal of the Spirit is described – *chrisma*, *sphragis* and *arrabōn* – John employs the first as most appropriate to his purpose[52] of assuring his readers that they suffer no disadvantage as compared with the 'inner ring': 'You, no less than they, are among the initiated; this is the gift of the Holy One, and by it you all have knowledge' (NEB).

NEB 'you all', like RV margin and RSV, follows the reading *pantes* (nominative plural masculine), whereas RV text, 'ye know all things', follows the reading *panta* (accusative plural neuter). The latter is the majority reading, but the former has the weighty support of the early witnesses to the Alexandrian text-type.[53] In favour of *pantes* is the fact that it is the more difficult reading (an object is normally expected after the verb 'know') and therefore more likely to be changed to *panta* than *vice versa*. Against this, it has been suggested that the reading *pantes* may have been influenced by the occurrence of the same word in verse 19 ('*they all are not of us*'). The reading *panta* ('all things') could be understood in the same sense as verse 27, 'his anointing teaches you about everything'.[54]

If we adopt the reading 'you all know' here, the point is that the true knowledge is not confined to a favoured élite but is accessible to them all. What they all know is made clear by the words that follow: they know the difference between truth and falsehood. They know the difference between these not because they have explored the mazes of falsehood but because they 'know the truth'.[55] For believers this 'truth' is embodied in a person, in Him who said 'I am . . . the truth' (John 14. 6). They know it because they know Him, and this knowledge is theirs because they have received 'the Spirit of truth' (John 14. 17; 15. 26; 16. 13). When He comes, said Jesus of the Spirit, 'he will guide you into all the truth' (John 16. 13), and to the same effect He prayed for His disciples: 'Sanctify them in the truth; thy word is truth' (John 17. 17). Those who have come to know the truth 'as the truth is in Jesus' (Eph. 4. 21) have, it is implied, a built-in spiritual instinct which enables them to detect and refuse whatever is basically incompatible with that truth, no matter how speciously and eloquently it may be set before them. They know that 'no lie is of the truth' – or, to quote the NEB rendering again: 'lies, one and all, are alien to the truth'.

So contrary to the truth of the gospel, so subversive of the saving message, is this 'lie' that it must be stamped as the teaching of Antichrist. Some two decades later John's disciple Polycarp, bishop of Smyrna, echoes his teacher's language: 'Every one who does not confess that Jesus Christ has come in the flesh is Antichrist. And whosoever does not confess the testimony of the cross is of the devil; and whosoever perverts the oracles of the Lord to his own lusts and says that there is neither resurrection nor judgment – he is Satan's firstborn'[56] By 'the testimony of the cross' Polycarp appears to mean the witness which our Lord's passion and death bore to Him as the incarnate Son of God (cf. John 19. 35; 1 John 5. 8).

V. 22 Who is the liar but that he denieth that Jesus is the Christ? This is the antichrist, *even* **he that denieth the Father and the Son. v. 23 Whosoever denieth the Son, the same hath not the Father: he that confesseth the Son hath the Father also.**

'Lies, one and all, are alien to the truth'; but John, like Paul in 2 Thess. 2. 11,[57] is thinking of one fundamental Lie. Plato made a distinction between those lies which are errors of fact and the mortal disease of 'the lie in the soul';[58] to John the Lie *par excellence* is that which refuses to see the Godhead shine in the human life and death of Jesus, that which drives a wedge between 'the Christ' and the man Jesus of whom, according to Cerinthus, 'the Christ' took temporary possession.[59] To deny that Jesus is the Christ is to deny that He 'is the Son of God' (5. 5) or that He 'has come in the flesh' (4. 2). This denial is deadly, because only in the Christ, the Son of God, who came in the flesh is eternal life to be had (5. 11).

The false teachers who perverted the received teaching about Jesus as the Christ and Son of God probably did not expressly deny *the Father*. Indeed, 'the Father' was the designation that many of them reserved for the God who is above all, in contradistinction to the inferior deity whom they envisaged as creator of the world.[60] According to Cerinthus, it was after 'the Christ' descended on the man Jesus at His baptism in the form of a dove that 'He proclaimed the unknown Father'.[61] But words have value only in accordance with their meaning; the Cerinthians and those like-minded might speak of the 'Father' but they did not give the same meaning to the term as John does when he speaks of 'the Father'. To John, the Father is He who has revealed Himself uniquely and fully in the incarnate Jesus, not only in the ministry of word and work for which He was anointed by the Spirit at His baptism, but equally so – indeed, supremely so – in His death on the cross.

Those who denied the incarnation of the Son of God and saw no revelatory element in His passion refused that revelation of the Father which is imparted in the gospel. In denying the Son, they denied the Father too, little as they may have intended to do so. This is a corollary to the repeated assertion in the Gospel of John, that the knowledge of the Father is inseparable from the knowledge of the Son (John 8. 19; 14. 7), and to a passage like John 5. 23, where the divine purpose in the committal of judgment to the Son is said to be 'that all may honour the Son, even as they honour the Father. He who does not honour the Son does not honour the Father who sent him'. 'The only Son,[62] who is in the bosom of the Father, he has made him known' (John 1. 18); to deny the Son is to deny the knowledge of the Father which He unfolds, and so to deny the Father Himself. This is not to exclude those prior and preparatory forms of divine revelation implied in the prologue to the Gospel of John;[63] it is to affirm that those earlier forms of divine revelation were brought to perfection when the Eternal Word became incarnate in the Son, so that it is no longer possible to confess the Father except as He has made Himself known in the Son, while it is impossible to believe in the Son without acknowledging the Father whom He has made known.[64] Whether Jesus expressed Himself in the imperative or in the indicative mood when He said, 'Believe in God, believe also in me'[65] (John 14. 1), He spoke essentially of one form of belief, not two.

V. 24   **As for you, let that abide in you which ye heard from the beginning. If that which ye heard from the beginning abide in you, ye also shall abide in the Son, and in the Father.**

'What you heard from the beginning' is the apostolic message as it was first delivered to them, as we have seen already in verse 7. Like the Gospel of John (cf. John 5. 38; 15. 7), so the Epistles can speak interchangeably of the word of God or of Christ 'abiding' in men (1 John 2. 14; 2 John 2) and of their 'abiding' in it (2 John 9). Either way, it is faithful adherence to the message that is intended, and this carries with it faithful adherence to the Father and the Son to whom in that message the Spirit bears witness. This personal relation with the Godhead is similarly mutual: those who 'abide' in God have God 'abiding' in them (cf. 1 John 4. 12–16). But those who have abandoned the foundation of their faith in the original apostolic testimony have severed themselves from fellowship with the true God, for that is the true testimony to God (cf. 1 John 5. 9–11).

V. 25 **And this is the promise which he promised [1]us,** *even* **the life eternal.**

[1] Some ancient authorities read *you*.

Eternal life is the promise held out to believers by God in the message which makes Him known; it is embodied, as has been made plain in 1 John 1. 2, in the Son of God who is the centre and circumference of that message. The original force of the phrase, especially in the Hebrew or Aramaic expressions which underlie the Greek *zōē aiōnios*, relates to 'the life of the age to come', i.e. resurrection life. But for those who are united by faith to Him who by His triumph over death is 'the resurrection and the life' (John 11. 25), the promise of resurrection life is already realized; they enjoy it here and now. John's readers will do well if they hold fast to the message and remain in the fellowship, without which eternal life is unattainable. If eternal life consists in the knowledge of the only true God and Jesus Christ whom He has sent (John 17. 3), then it cannot be dissociated from the message which conveys that knowledge.

V. 26 **These things have I written unto you concerning them that would lead you astray.** v. 27 **And as for you, the anointing which ye received of him abideth in you, and ye need not that any one teach you; but as his anointing teacheth you concerning all things, [1]and is true, and is no lie, and even as it taught you, [2]ye abide in him.**

[1] Or, *so it is true, and is no lie; and even as &c.*
[2] Or, *abide ye.*

'I have written' is the aorist tense (Gr. *egrapsa*), as in verses 13c–14 and 21. Once again we may recognize the 'epistolary aorist', or perhaps the reference here is to what has just been written about the 'many antichrists'. The most effective safeguard which the readers have against these people and their teaching is that 'anointing from the Holy One' already mentioned in verse 20 which enables them to recognize the truth and refuse falsehood. The fact that they have not followed the teachers of error in their secession is a token that this 'anointing' remains in them. The statement that because of it they do not need any one to teach them is to be understood in its context. It is not to be taken as absolute affirmation that the experience of the Spirit in personal life carries with it independence of the ministry of teaching in the church. The ministry of teaching is the Spirit's gift by which He provides instruction for believers. What is John himself doing in this letter if he is not 'teaching' his readers? But the ministry of teaching must be exercised by men who themselves share the 'anointing' of which John speaks, men who remain in the fellowship of the Spirit. No one from outside that fellowship – and the false teachers had placed themselves outside it – can provide teaching which will either correct or supplement the truth of the Christian revelation. The believers to whom John writes have not become so impoverished within their fellowship that they need any one from outside it to teach them. It is within the fellowship that the Spirit operates; it is there that He teaches the people of God. So Paul prays that those who are inwardly strengthened by the Spirit of Christ 'may have power to comprehend *with all the saints* what is the breadth and length and height and depth' (Eph. 3. 18). In the period before the canon of the New Testament began to circulate as a documentary collection, oral ministry was even more necessary than afterwards as the means by which the Spirit guided believers 'into all the truth'. They had their sacred scriptures in the books of the Old Testament, but these books had to be understood in the light of their fulfilment by Jesus, and a great part of early Christian teaching consisted in the imparting of this understanding. The Spirit by whom the prophets spoke was the Spirit by whose illumination the words of the prophets were understood (1 Pet. 1. 10–12).

In assuring his readers that the Spirit's 'anointing' teaches them about 'all things', John echoes the promise to the disciples in John 14. 26: 'the Counsellor, the Holy Spirit, ... will teach you all things'. The apostolic teaching which the readers have already received represents the fulfilment of this promise. Here is the truth; whatever contradicts it is falsehood. Those who have been taught it will do well to adhere to it, to 'abide' in the Spirit's anointing as that anointing 'abides' in them.

It is not completely clear whether we are to understand the anointing or the Spirit in the last two clauses of verse 27. RV text, following AV and followed by RSV, makes the anointing ('it') subject of 'taught' but takes *en autō* at the end of the verse to refer to the Spirit ('in him'), not to the anointing ('in it', which is also a permissible rendering). Since 'the anointing' is the subject of the earlier part of the sentence, we might well retain it throughout: 'as it has taught you, abide in it'. NEB, on the other hand, sees the Spirit in both of the two last clauses: 'As he taught you, then, dwell in him'. Certainty is not attainable; practically it makes no difference, since the anointing is the Spirit's anointing.

5 CHILDREN OF GOD (2. 28–3. 24)

When John in this epistle addresses his readers as his 'children', he uses the diminutive form *teknia* (except, as we have seen, for two places in Chapter 2 – verses 13 and 18 – where he calls them *paidia*), but when he calls them 'children of God' he uses the plural *tekna* (the form of which *teknia* is the diminutive). The phrase *tekna tou theou* occurs similarly for 'children of God' in the Gospel (John 1. 12; 11. 52). When speaking of believers' relationship to God, John never uses the noun *hyios* ('son'); he reserves it for Christ, as the unique (*monogenēs*) Son of God.[66] The words used to denote relationship to God carry with them also the connotation of likeness to God; the two ideas are inseparable, for likeness is the proof of relationship.

(a) The two families (2. 28–3. 10)

Some students of this epistle have discerned behind these verses an earlier document consisting of a series of antitheses,[67] e.g.:

(i) Every one who does right is born of him/
    Every one who commits sin is guilty of lawlessness (2. 29/3.4)
(ii) No one who abides in him sins/
    No one who sins has either seen him or known him (3. 6a/b)
(iii) He who does right is righteous/
    He who commits sin is of the devil (3. 7/3. 8)
(iv) No one born of God commits sin/
    Whoever does not do right is not of God (3. 9/3. 10)

This identification of an earlier document, no longer extant, be-hind an existing document is a precarious exercise. But it is a perfectly reasonable, and even probable, supposition that the Elder, in his teaching, whether oral or written, was accustomed to sum up the contrast between the true way and all others in pairs of antitheses like these. As previously, so here he insists on the ethical criteria of the true way; no amount of profession will compensate for their absence.

V. 28   And now, *my* little children, abide in him; that, if he shall be manifested, we may have boldness, and not be ashamed [1]before him at his [2]coming.

[1] Gr. from him.   [2] Gr. presence.

The emphatic 'And now' (Gr. *kai nyn*) introduces a new thought. Even if 'abide in it' were the right rendering at the end of verse 27, the same clause at the beginning of verse 28 is cer-tainly to be understood personally, 'abide in him'. There is no material difference; those who 'abide' in the 'anointing' and in the teaching which accompanies it are bound to 'abide' in Christ (cf. John 15. 4). Those who 'abide in him' can look forward to His coming with joy; they 'have confidence for the day of judgment' (4. 17, RSV). This is the only place in the Johannine writings where the word *parousia* ('advent') is used; but the idea that it expresses is frequently conveyed by other terms, as in this very context by the clause 'if he shall be manifested'. Neither here nor in the repetition of the clause in 3.2 does 'if' suggest any uncertainty; it is the equivalent of 'when'. 'The life which was manifested' (1. 2) will be manifested again. The first person plural in 'we may have boldness' . . . is probably the inclusive 'we', meaning 'we and you together'. Attempts have been made to interpret the passage as though it meant '*You* must abide in Him, in order that *we* (your teachers) may have confidence and not be ashamed . . .' (a similar sentiment to Paul's in Phil. 2.16; 1 Thess. 2.19 f., etc.); but in that case we should have expected the contrast between the pronouns to be expressed more emphatically, as it is in 1.3. Here as elsewhere John takes away the ground from any antinomian perversion of the gospel; what else could an unfaithful servant do than 'shrink in shame'[68] (cf. RSV) from his Master's searching eye? 'Boldness' ('freedom of speech')[69] in the Lord's presence is the antithesis to such shame.

V. 29 If ye know that he is righteous, [1]ye know that every one also that doeth righteousness is begotten of him.

[1] Or, *know ye.*

That God is righteous is a biblical axiom: 'the LORD is righteous, he loves righteous deeds' (Ps. 11. 7). In Old Testament times He required righteousness in His people because they were called by His name: 'righteousness, righteousness you shall follow' (to give the literal rendering of Deut. 16. 20). In the teaching of our Lord, not least in the Sermon on the Mount, it is emphasized that the children[70] of the heavenly Father will reproduce His character (Matt. 5. 45, 48; Luke 6. 35 f.). So John makes it clear that membership in the family of God is to be recognized by the family likeness; since the Father of the family is righteous, the children will practise righteousness. If anyone claims to belong to His family and does not practise righteousness, his claim cannot be admitted; anyone who practises righteousness is known by that very fact to be a child of God, even if he makes no such claim in words. Actions speak louder than words.[71]

NOTES

1. In 1 John 2. 12, 28; 3. 7, 18; 4. 4; 5. 21. Where *teknia* is not accompanied by the possessive pronoun 'my' (Gr. *mou*), as it is in 2. 1, RV in this epistle distinguishes it by adding this pronoun in italics: '*my* little children'.

2. It appears as a variant reading to *teknia* in 1 John 3. 7.

3. In these epistles *teknon* occurs in 1 John 3. 1, 2, 10 (twice); 5. 2; 2 John 1, 4, 13; 3 John 4 (always in the plural).

4. E.g. in the *Similitudes of Enoch* (1 Enoch 38. 2, etc.).

5. The form *paraklētos* is a verbal adjective from *parakaleō*. The AV and RV rendering 'Comforter' in the Gospel passages gives it an active force, relating it to the sense 'comfort' or 'encourage' which the verb frequently has (cf. Matt. 2. 18; 5. 4; Luke 16. 25; 2 Cor. 1. 4, 6). But its force is more probably passive (as is usual with such verbal adjectives), related to the sense 'call to one's side (as a helper)'; cf. Latin *ad-uocatus*, whence our 'advocate'. In this sense *paraklētos* was taken over as a loanword into Mishnaic Hebrew, in the form *pĕraqlîṭ*, 'advocate', 'intercessor'.

6. E.g. in Heb. 7. 25.

7. For the relevance of the NEB rendering see p. 46, n. 18.

8. This was the force of these words (associated with the verb *hilaskomai*, 'propitiate') in pagan Greek. But the NT force of this word-group is based on its use in the Septuagint to render the Hebrew word-group associated with the verb *kipper* ('atone'), in which God, far from being the object, takes the initiative. Cf. Rom. 3. 25, where it is God who has set Jesus forth as a propitiation by means of His blood – i.e. His sacrificial death (cf. pp. 43 f.); the word there rendered 'propitiation' (Gr. *hilastērion*) is the same as is used in the Septuagint (cf. Heb. 9. 5) to render Heb. *kappōreth*, 'mercy-seat', 'place (or means) of propitiation'. The object of the propitiatory action is men's sins, as in Heb. 2. 17, where 'sins' (Gr. *hamartias*) is in the accusative case after the infinitive *hilaskesthai* ('to make atonement for', 'to expiate').

9. Cf. Heb. 10. 19: 'we have confidence to enter the sanctuary by the blood of Jesus'.

10. For the world (*kosmos*) as the object of Christ's saving work cf. 1 John 4. 14; also John 3. 16, 17; 4. 42; 12. 47. John Calvin, in commenting on the present passage, agrees that 'Christ suffered sufficiently for the whole world but effectively only for the elect' but denies (no doubt rightly) that this is John's meaning here (*Commentary on John 11–21 and 1 John*, trans. T. H. L. Parker, Edinburgh, 1961, p. 244).

11. So magnificent a composition that for the sake of the rest of it I can even bring myself to sing 'My God is reconciled' – provided I may treat 'reconciled' as an adjective, describing God's attitude to mankind, and not as a participle, as though the sacrifice of Christ produced a change in His nature.

12. The other two occurrences are 1 John 3. 5 ('*he* was manifested . . .'), 16 ('*he* laid down his life . . .').

13. The verb 'abide' (Gr. *menō*), in addition to its ordinary usage, appears frequently in the Johannine Gospel and Epistles with a distinctive sense, setting forth the mutual coinherence of the believer in Christ (and in the Father) and of Christ (and the Father) in the believer. Paul does not use the verb in this sense, but occasionally expresses a similar idea by means of *oikeō*, *enoikeō*, *katoikeō*, 'dwell' (cf. Rom. 8. 9, 11; 1 Cor. 3. 16; 2 Cor. 6. 16; Eph. 3. 17), and in one well-known passage by means of *zaō*, 'live' (Gal. 2. 20: 'it is no longer I who live, but Christ who lives in me'), but more

often without the use of any verb, in such phrases as 'in Christ', 'Christ in you'. The quotation from Epimenides in Acts 17. 28 ('In him we live and move and have our being') presents a formal parallel, but there it is physical life that is meant.

14. See note on 1 John 1. 5 (pp. 40f.). W. Dittenberger quotes a Greek inscription (dated AD 515/6) from the Church of St. George in Zorava, Syria (in allusion to its having been built where a pagan temple once stood): 'The saving light has shone, where darkness once concealed' (*Orientis Graeci Inscriptiones Selectae*, Leipzig, 1905, No. 610, 2).

15. This is the force of the present tense *paragetai* (used also of 'the world' in verse 17).

16. E. Percy, *John Knox* (London, 1937), pp. 73 f.

17. Cf. John 11. 9 f.; 12. 35 f., quoted in the note on 1 John 1. 6 (pp. 42 f.).

18. Cf. 1 John 3. 10 ff.; 4. 7 ff.

19. This is more probable than the view that these terms in verses 12 and 13c also apply to the whole body of John's readers, who are then subdivided into 'fathers' and 'young men'.

20. See p. 83, n. 66.

21. See p. 143 with p. 145, n. 29.

22. Gr. *ap' archēs*, as in Mic. 5. 2, LXX (see p. 45, n. 1).

23. Cf. John 16. 33.

24. Cf. 1 John 4. 4; 5. 4 f.

25. Cf. the promises to the 'overcomer' in the Letters to the Seven Churches (Rev. 2. 7, 11, 17, 26; 3. 5, 12, 21) and in Rev. 21. 7; also Rev. 5. 5; 12. 11; 15. 2.

26. 'The evil one' (Gr. *ho ponēros*) appears several times in NT as a designation of the devil or the tempter, especially in Matthew; e.g. in the Lord's Prayer (Matt. 6. 13) and in the interpretation of the parables of the Sower (Matt. 13. 19) and of the Tares (Matt. 13. 38). In John 17. 15 our Lord prays that His disciples may be kept 'from the evil one'. Cf. 1 John 3. 12; 5. 18 f.

27. The distinction between *logos* and *rhēma* should not be overpressed; cf. John 8. 31, 'if you abide (*menō*) in my word (*logos*), you are truly my disciples', and 15. 7 f., 'if . . . my words (*rhēmata*) abide in you, . . . so shall you be my disciples'.

28. The 'world' in this sense corresponds to the 'darkness' of verse 8 (see note on p. 55). Compare Paul's language about 'the present evil age (*aiōn*)' in Gal. 1. 4 and the Qumran description of the current era as 'the epoch of wickedness' (*Damascus Rule* 6. 10, etc.).

29. Cf. the NEB paraphrase: 'Everything the world affords, all that panders to the appetites, or entices the eyes, all the glamour of its life'.

30. In 2 Pet. 2. 14 the lust of the eyes has a sexual connotation (cf. Matt. 5. 29), but that is not necessarily so here.

31. On John's use here of Gr. *alazoneia* (RV 'vainglory') E. K. Simpson says: 'He is contemplating the unregenerate world as a Vanity Fair, and the full strength of his expression can be brought out only by some such translation as the *charlatanry* or *make-believe* of life' (*Words Worth Weighing in the Greek New Testament*, London, 1946, p. 18). Cf. the same word in Jas. 4. 16: 'you boast in your *arrogance*' (RSV).

32. F. Holmes, *Brother Indeed* (London, 1956), p. 37.

33. Cf. pp. 15 f., 25 f.

34. Gr. *paragetai*, as in verse 8. In 1 Cor. 7. 31 Paul uses the active voice *paragei*

intransitively in the same sense. Cf. 2 Cor. 4. 18: 'the things that are seen are transient'.

35. See note on 2. 1 (p. 48).

36. J. H. Newman, 'Waiting for Christ', *Parochial and Plain Sermons*, vi (London, 1896), p. 241.

37. The resumptive adverb 'now' is more naturally construed with 'you know' than (as in RSV) with 'what is restraining him'. W. Kelly stigmatizes the latter construction as a solecism (*The Epistles to the Thessalonians*,³ London, 1953, p. 146).

38. 2 Thess. 2. 3–10.

39. That the 'abomination' is personal in Mark 13. 14 is indicated by the choice of the masculine participle 'standing' (Gr. *hestēkota*) although the noun which it qualifies is in the neuter gender (*bdelygma*). Cf. NEB: 'when you see "the abomination of desolation" usurping a place which is not his'.

40. Dan. 9. 27; 11. 31; 12. 11.

41. 1 Macc. 1. 41–61 (especially verse 54: 'on the fifteenth day of Chislev, in the one hundred and forty-fifth year [i.e. of the Seleucid era, beginning 312 BC], they erected an "abomination of desolation" [i.e. a pagan altar] on the altar of burnt-offering').

42. Philo, *Embassy to Gaius*, 203 ff., Josephus, *War* ii. 184 ff., *Antiquities* xviii. 261 ff.

43. Josephus, *War* vi. 316.

44. 2 Cor. 6. 15; the word, used in the sense of 'death' or 'hell' in OT (cf. Ps. 18. 4 f., where it appears in synonymous parallelism with 'death' and 'Sheol'), is employed in this personal way in the Qumran texts and other Jewish and Christian literature of the late BC and early AD epoch.

45. Literally 'enmity', used personally (like Belial/Beliar) in the Qumran texts and other Jewish and Christian literature of this period.

46. Theodotion's Greek version of the OT, intended to replace the 'Septuagint' for Jewish use, appeared late in the second century AD; his version of Daniel was so far superior to the older, paraphrastic 'Septuagint' version that it was adopted by Greek-speaking Christians. It seems, however, to have been based on an earlier, non-Septuagintal, version with which some of the NT writers were acquainted.

47. They are thus interpreted in the earliest surviving full-scale exposition of the doctrine of Antichrist in Christian literature – Hippolytus's treatise *On Antichrist* (*c.* AD 200).

48. For a detailed exegetical study of this doctrine see I. H. Marshall, *Kept by the Power of God* (London, 1969); the evidence of the Epistles of John is examined on pp. 183 ff.

49. Cf. John 1. 8, 31; 3. 17; 9. 3; 11. 52; 12. 47; 13. 18; 14. 31; 15. 25.

50. 'The Inner Ring', in *Transposition and Other Addresses* (London, 1949), pp. 55 ff.; *Screwtape Proposes a Toast and Other Pieces* (London, 1965), pp. 28 ff.

51. Jesus Himself is said similarly to have been 'anointed . . . with the Holy Spirit' (Acts 10. 38; cf. Isa. 61. 1 in the light of 11. 2; 42. 1); this is probably a reference to the descent of the dove at His baptism (Mark 1. 10, etc.).

52. Perhaps because the seceders laid claim to a special 'anointing' (*chrisma*) which admitted them to esoteric 'knowledge' (*gnōsis*, a noun never used in the Johannine literature, surprisingly but no doubt designedly). In the following century the members of the gnostic sect of the Naassenes claimed: 'we alone of all men are Christians, for we complete the mystery at the third gate and are anointed there with unspeakable chrism' (Hippolytus,

Refutation of Heresies v. 9. 22). Cf. the anointing of Aseneth mentioned on p. 131, n. 11.

53. Especially Codices Sinaiticus and Vaticanus and the Sahidic Coptic version.

54. T. W. Manson, following A. Harnack, states his preference for 'all things', partly on the ground that *oida* ('I know') 'is not used absolutely in the Fourth Gospel or the Johannine Epistles', and refers to John 14. 26 ('Entry into Membership of the Early Church', *JTS* 48, 1947, p. 28, n. 1).

55. The tense of 'I have . . . written' in verse 21 is the epistolary aorist (*egrapsa*), as in verses 13c and 14.

56. *To the Philippians* 7. 1. The expression 'Satan's firstborn' seems to have been a favourite of Polycarp's: many years later (AD 154), when Polycarp was on a visit to Rome, the heresiarch Marcion is said to have sought an interview with him and asked the aged bishop if he recognized him, to which he received the answer, 'I recognize – Satan's firstborn!' (Irenaeus, *Against Heresies* iii. 3. 4).

57. Where God sends 'a strong delusion' on those who refused the love of the saving truth, so that instead they believe 'the Lie'. Cf. Rom. 1. 25, where disobedient mankind 'exchanged the truth about God for the Lie'. In the teaching of Zoroaster 'The Lie' (Avestan *druj*) denotes the whole system of evil.

58. *Republic* ii. 382 b–c.

59. See pp. 16 f.

60. This is plain, for example, in the later *Gospel of Thomas* (a compilation of sayings of Jesus with a gnosticizing tendency), where the supreme Being, proclaimed by Jesus, is called 'the Father', whereas the designation 'God' is reserved for an inferior power.

61. See p. 17.

62. So RSV text. But the reading which is relegated to the margin of RSV (as of RV, ARV and NEB), 'God only-begotten, who has his being in the Father's bosom . . .', has strong external and internal support.

63. The Divine Word was in the world in various ways before 'becoming flesh' and so communicating the fullness of God's glory (John 1. 9–14); cf. the 'many and various ways' in which God spoke to men before 'in these last days' He spoke His definitive word in the Son (Heb. 1. 1 f.).

64. There is no valid ground for the italicization in AV of the second part of verse 23; although these words 'he who confesses the Son has the Father also' are absent from later manuscripts and from the 'Received Text', they are well attested in our major authorities.

65. The repeated form *pisteuete* is identical in both moods.

66. Paul uses *tekna* ('children') and *hyioi* ('sons') indiscriminately to denote Christians' relationship to God, as an examination of Rom. 8. 14–21 shows, though he prefers *hyioi* (as in Gal. 3. 26–4. 7), perhaps because of its presence in the compound *hyiothesia*, 'adoption' (see note on 2. 12 ff., p. 58). A near exception in the Johannine usage is the phrase *hyioi phōtos*, 'sons of light', in John 12. 36, but this was probably a stereotyped phrase (cf. Luke 16. 8; 1 Thess. 5. 5, although Eph. 5. 8 has *tekna phōtos*).

67. Cf. W. Nauck, *Die Tradition und der Charakter des ersten Johannesbriefes* (Tübingen, 1957), pp. 1 ff. Somewhat similar is P. Carrington's working out of a primitive Christian catechism in 1 John 3 (*The Primitive Christian Catechism*, Cambridge, 1940, pp. 19 ff.).

68. Gr. *aischynomai apo*, a construction not found elsewhere in NT. It occurs five times in LXX, but never quite in the same sense as here (usually the noun

following *apo* denotes something or someone of which the subject of the
verb is rightly ashamed). The nearest parallel is Sir. 21. 22: 'The foot of a
fool rushes into a house, but a man of experience stands respectfully before
it (*aischynthēsetai apo prosōpou*).'

69. Gr. *parrhēsia*; cf. 3. 21; 4. 17; 5. 14.
70. In Matt. 5. 45 and Luke 6. 35 the word used is *hyioi* ('sons'); those who
press a distinction between this and *tekna* should reflect that in Hebrew or
Aramaic no such distinction is possible; one and the same word (*bnê*,
construct plural) must be envisaged behind either rendering.
71. As RV margin indicates, the verb *ginōskete* may be imperative as well as
indicative. RSV ('you may be sure . . .') and NEB ('you must recognize . . .')
probably present free renderings of the imperative.

CHAPTER III

V. 1 Behold what manner of love the Father hath bestowed upon us, that we should be called children of God: and *such* we are. For this cause the world knoweth us not, because it knew him not. v. 2 Beloved, now are we children of God, and it is not yet made manifest what we shall be. We know that, if ¹he shall be manifested, we shall be like him; for we shall see him even as he is.

¹ Or, *it.*

This language echoes that of the Prologue to the Gospel, where the Eternal Logos receives no welcome among those who should be first to acknowledge him: 'but to all who received him, who believed in his name, he gave power to become children of God; who were born . . . of God' (John 1. 12, 13). Here, however, God's calling believers His children is a token of the greatness of His love for them. A parallel statement in a Jewish context is ascribed to Rabbi Akiba (died AD 135): 'Beloved is man, for he was created in the image of God, but by a special love it was made known to him that he was created in the image of God, as it is said, "For in the image of God made he man" (Gen. 9. 6). Beloved are Israel, for they were called children of God, but by a special love it was made known to them that they were called children of God, as it is said, "You are children of the LORD your God" (Deut. 14. 1).'¹ The words 'and such we are', omitted in later manuscripts and in AV, remind us that when God calls, His call is effectual; people and things *are* what He calls them.

These first two verses of 1 John 3 celebrate the accomplishment of God's eternal purpose concerning man. This purpose finds expression in Gen. 1. 26, where God, about to bring into being the crown of creation, says: 'Let us make man in our image, after our likeness'. In other words, He declares His intention of bringing into existence beings like Himself, as like Himself as it is possible

85

for creatures to be like their Creator. In words which echo the language of Genesis 1, the status and function of man in the purpose of God are celebrated in Ps. 8. 5 ff.: 'thou hast made him little less than God, and dost crown him with glory and honour. Thou hast given him dominion over the works of thy hands; thou hast put all things under his feet'. But Genesis 3 tells how man, not content with the true likeness to God which was his by creation, grasped at the counterfeit likeness held out as the tempter's bait: 'you will be like God, knowing good and evil'. In consequence, things most *unlike* God manifested themselves in human life: hatred, darkness and death in place of love, light and life. The image of God in man was sadly defaced. Yet God's purpose was not frustrated; instead, the fall itself, with its entail of sin and death, was overruled by God and compelled to become an instrument in the furtherance of His purpose.

In the fullness of time the image of God, undefaced by disobedience to His will, reappeared on earth in the person of His Son. In Jesus the love, light and life of God were manifested in opposition to hatred, darkness and death. With His crucifixion it seemed that hatred, darkness and death had won the day, and that God's purpose, which had survived the fall, was now effectively thwarted. But instead, the cross of Jesus proved to be God's chosen instrument for the fulfilment of His purpose. 'To this end was the Son of God manifested, that he might destroy the works of the devil' (1 John 3. 8), and it was by His cross that He did so (cf. Col. 2. 14 f.). The last Adam by His obedience has restored what the first Adam by his disobedience forfeited and has ensured the triumph of God's purpose. This purpose is stated by Paul in terms which go back far beyond the act of creation in Genesis 1: 'those whom he foreknew he also predestined to be conformed to the image of his Son, in order that he might be the first-born among many brethren' (Rom. 8. 29). The children of God, who enter His family through faith in His Son, display their Father's likeness, because of their conformity to Him who is the perfect image of the invisible God. They display it in measure here and now; they will display it fully on a coming day, for 'we know that, if he shall be manifested, we shall be like him; for we shall see him even as he is'. The consummation of God's purpose in man coincides with the advent of Christ in glory: then those who 'have borne the image of the man of dust' will 'bear the image of the man of heaven' (1 Cor. 15. 49); the new man, who at present 'is being renewed in knowledge after the image of his Creator' (Col. 3. 10), will have come to full maturity. When Christ, His people's life, is manifested, they will be manifested with Him in glory (Col. 3. 4), so that the day of His appearing is also the day of 'the revealing of the sons of God' (Rom. 8. 19). Sonship is present, but vision is future.[2]

Referring to the present work of sanctification, Paul says that the people of Christ, beholding His glory and then reflecting it 'as in a mirror', are 'transfigured into his likeness' (2 Cor. 3. 18, NEB). If progressive assimilation to the likeness of their Lord results from their present beholding of Him through a glass darkly, to behold Him face to face, to 'see him even as he is', will result in their being perfectly like Him.

In the sentence, 'For this cause the world knoweth us not, because it knew him not', the pronoun 'him' probably refers to 'the Father', since He is the only one mentioned in the singular in the preceding sentence; otherwise we might think of the world's failure to recognize or welcome the Son of God when He came. But it is a matter of small moment; the reception given to the Son is reckoned as given to the Father too: 'If I had not done among them the works which no one else did, they would not have sin', says Jesus to His disciples in the upper room; 'but now they have seen and hated both me and my Father' (John 15. 24). Similarly our Lord forewarned His disciples that the reception given to Him would equally be given to them.[3]

Before moving on from verse 2, it may be well to make passing reference to the NEB rendering: 'what we shall be has not yet been disclosed, but we know that when it is disclosed we shall be like him, because we shall see him as he is'. Here the subject of the clause which RV renders 'if he shall be manifested' is taken to be not 'he' but 'it' (cf. RV margin), harking back to 'what we shall be'.[4]

This is a perfectly permissible rendering, but it is better to understand a personal subject, as in NEB margin, where 'when he appears' is given as an alternative rendering to 'when it is disclosed' of the text. NEB suggests yet another rendering in a further marginal note: 'we are God's children, though he has not yet appeared; what we shall be we know, for when he does appear we shall be like him'. This presupposes a different punctuation from the other renderings, but on the whole the familiar punctuation seems to be more satisfactory.

V. 3 And every one that hath this hope *set* on him purifieth himself, even as he is pure.

The use of the preposition 'on' (Gr. *epi*) after the noun 'hope' makes it sufficiently certain that 'him' means Christ, or God in Christ. The AV 'every man that hath this hope in him' is ambiguous; it might be taken to mean 'everyone who has this hope (implanted) in himself', whereas the pronoun following *epi* must denote the object of the hope.[5] As in 2. 6 and two other places in this letter,[6] 'he' in the phrase 'as he' represents Gr. *ekeinos* and denotes Christ. Christ Himself is pure – He is indeed the very norm of purity – and a hope that rests 'on him' cannot but have a purifying effect in the life of the one who so hopes. For to have one's hope set on Christ implies that He is a constant object of meditation and contemplation; when that is so, the words of Paul come true, that 'we all, with unveiled face, beholding the glory of the Lord, are being changed into his likeness from one degree of glory to another' (2 Cor. 3. 18). This is the proper preparation for the day when His people's conformity to His likeness will be consummated, when, at His appearing, they become completely 'like him', because then they will 'see him as he is'. Here and now they are urged 'to lead a life worthy of the calling' with which God has called them (Eph. 4. 1), and since that calling involves their ultimately being glorified with Christ (Rom. 8. 28–30), present likeness to Christ is indispensable to a life worthy of that calling. 'Blessed are the pure in heart, for they shall see God' (Matt. 5. 8).

V. 4   Every one that doeth sin doeth also lawlessness: and sin is lawlessness.

The practising of sin is the opposite of the practising of righteousness which, as John has said in 2. 29, characterizes those who have been born into God's family. Lest someone in the opposite camp should interrupt at this point in order to discuss theoretically what is and what is not the nature of sin, John cuts him short with a terse definition, which is adequate for his practical purpose: 'sin is lawlessness'. The seceders' 'new morality' took little account of divine law or of sin against it; John insists that sin, in the common sense of the term, is rebellion against God. The AV rendering, 'sin is the transgression of the law' (taken over from the Geneva Bible), is unfortunate, since it suggests the contravention of this or that specific law rather than a generally lawless attitude towards God. 'Sin is not transgression of law but lawlessness, and lawlessness is sin. It is a convertible or reciprocating proposition, the subject being identified with the predicate.'[7]

V. 5   And ye know that he was manifested to [1]take away sins; and in him is no sin. v. 6 Whosoever abideth in him sinneth not: whosoever sinneth hath not seen him, neither [2]knoweth him.

[1] Or, *bear sins*.   [2] Or, *hath known*.

The noun sins' is preceded in the original by the definite article. If we include the article in a literal translation, '*he* (the emphatic *ekeinos*[8]) was manifested to take away the sins', the question arises, 'What sins?' – to which the answer is 'Ours'. (In fact some manuscripts, including Codex Sinaiticus, with the Sahidic Coptic and Syriac Peshitta, add the pronoun, making '*our* sins' quite explicit.) In John 1. 29 Jesus is proclaimed by the Baptist to be 'the Lamb of God, who takes away the *sin* of the world' in the singular; here the plural 'sins' has in view the individual sins of His people,[9] as in 2. 2, where he is called 'the propitiation for our sins'. The taking away of sins can be accomplished only by one who is himself sinless; hence the reminder:

'in him is no sin'. This goes further than to say that He committed no sin; it denies the presence of indwelling sin in His heart, and approximates to Paul's designation of Him in 2 Cor. 5. 21 as the One 'who knew no sin' (i.e. had no consciousness of it in His personal experience). If, then, He appeared on earth to take away His people's sins and is Himself the sinless One, how can sin be cherished by anyone who 'abides' in Him? In saying that no one who 'abides' in him sins, John is not asserting that it is impossible for a believer to commit an occasional act of sin. He has already pointed to the provision made for such an emergency by means of confession (1. 9) and Christ's activity as His people's Advocate (2. 1 f.), and has warned his readers against unfounded claims to be sinless within or without (1. 8, 10). What he does assert is that a sinful life does not mark a child of God, so that anyone who leads such a life is shown thereby not to be a child of God. When a boy goes to a new school, he may inadvertently do something out of keeping with the school's tradition or good name, to be told immediately, 'That isn't done here'. A literalist might reply, 'But obviously it *is* done; this boy has just done it' – but he would be deliberately missing the point of the rebuke. The point of the rebuke is that such conduct is disapproved of in this school, so anyone who practises it can normally be assumed not to belong to the school. There may be odd exceptions, but that is the general rule, which has been verified by experience. Fellowship with the sinless One and indulgence in sin are a contradiction in terms. Whatever high claims may be made by one who indulges in sin, that indulgence is sufficient proof that he has no personal knowledge of Christ. So, in the Gospel of John, Jesus says to His disciples, 'If you had known me, you would have known my Father also; henceforth you know him and have seen him' (John 14. 7); to those who refused Him credence He says, 'His [the Father's] voice you have never heard, his form you have never seen; and you do not have his word abiding in you, for you do not believe in him whom he has sent . . . You know neither me nor my Father; if you knew me, you would know my Father also' (John 5. 37 f.; 8. 19). Similarly, in his letter to Gaius, John propounds the simple antithesis: 'He who does good is of God; he who does evil has not seen God' (3 John 11).

V. 7 *My* **little children, let no man lead you astray: he that doeth righteousness is righteous, even as he is righteous: v. 8 he that doeth sin is of the devil; for the devil sinneth from the beginning. To this end was the Son of God manifested, that he might destroy the works of the devil.**

The false teachers with their sophistry (cf. 2. 26) were capable not merely of condoning sin, but of making it seem virtuous. Against their arguments John's 'little children' (*teknia*) would be fortified if they remembered his plain, uncomplicated maxims. Behaviour is of unsurpassed importance in the Christian way. Believers are indeed justified before God by His grace, which they accept by faith; but those who have been justified thus will show it by their behaviour. Righteousness is as consonant with the character of Christ – since 'he (*ekeinos*) is righteous' – as sin is consonant with the character of the devil, who has been sinning, rebelling against God (this is the force of the Greek present here), ever since the beginning.[10] In the Gospel Jesus tells some people who boasted in their descent from Abraham that their behaviour proclaimed them to be children not of Abraham but of the devil, because the latter 'was a murderer from the beginning' (John 8. 44). Here the antithesis is between the family of God and the family of the devil; in either family the children may be known by their moral likeness to the head of the family. The very purpose of the Son of God's appearance on earth was 'to destroy the works of the devil' – 'destroy' renders Gr. *lyō*, here used in the same sense as it has in Eph. 2. 14, where Christ 'has broken down the middle wall of hostility'. Chief of the devil's works is sin, which the Son of God came to take away (cf. verse 5). How can one in whose life sin has manifestly not been destroyed or taken away claim to dwell in Christ? Is it not rather self-evident that he belongs to the family which is characterized by rebellion against God, and whose head is the arch-rebel?

V. 9   Whosoever is begotten of God doeth no sin, because his seed abideth in him: and he cannot sin, because he is begotten of God.

The first sentence of verse 9 repeats in substance the first sentence of verse 6: 'whosoever abides in him does not sin'. Once again, John emphasizes that the practice of sin is something that characterizes the children of him who 'has been sinning from the beginning' (v. 8), not the children of God. The reason the child of God does not practise sin is said to be that 'his seed abides in him' – a clause which can be understood in more than one way. That 'his seed' means God's seed is fairly certain. This may mean the divine nature implanted in the believer through the new birth; so RSV: 'God's nature abides in him' and thus prevents him from sinning (cf. NEB: 'the divine seed remains in him; he cannot be a sinner, because he is God's child').[11] But 'seed' is frequently used in the sense of 'offspring' (as, for example, in the discussion about Abraham's 'seed' in Gal. 3. 16–29); if that is the sense of the word here, then the meaning of the passage is not 'God's nature remains in the child of God' but 'God's child remains in God and cannot sin because he is *God's* offspring'. There is not much practical difference between the two constructions; the difference resides mainly in the precise force of the noun 'seed' and the reference of the pronoun 'him'. The latter construction might be regarded as an expansion of verse 6a.

One way or the other, the new birth involves a radical change in human nature; for those who have not experienced it, sin is natural, whereas for those who have experienced it, sin is unnatural – so unnatural, indeed, that its practice constitutes a powerful refutation of any claim to possess the divine life. John's antitheses are clear-cut. While they are to be understood in the context of his letter and of the situation which it presupposes, any attempt to weaken them, out of regard for human infirmity, or to make them less sharp and uncompromising than they are, is to misinterpret them. True interpretation must allow an author to mean what he says, even if that meaning is uncongenial to the interpreter.

V. 10 **In this the children of God are manifest, and the children of the devil: whosoever doeth not righteousness is not of God, neither he that loveth not his brother.**

In summing up the criteria which distinguish the two spiritual families one from the other, John adds love of one's brother to the practice of righteousness as a mark of the child of God, and the absence of such love, with the practice of unrighteousness, as a disqualification for membership in God's family. Righteousness by itself, while infinitely preferable to unrighteousness, might appear to be coldly judicial, but the addition of brotherly love (cf. 2. 9 f.) imparts a transforming warmth to John's exposition. For him, righteousness and love are inseparable; since they are inseparable in the character of God and in His revelation in Christ, so they must be inseparable in the lives of His people. If, slightly changing the lawyer's question in the Gospel story, we ask, 'And who is my brother?' the answer, especially in the light of verse 17 (p. 96), will be not unlike that which our Lord gave to 'Who is my neighbour?' – 'Any one who needs my love'.[12]

(b) The test of love (3. 11–18)

V. 11 **For this is the message which ye heard from the beginning, that we should love one another:** v. 12 **not as Cain was of the evil one, and slew his brother. And wherefore slew he him? Because his works were evil, and his brother's righteous.**

Love is an indispensable feature in the lives of the children of God, because it is the embodiment of the gospel message, and of the 'new commandment' which they received when first they were taught the Christian way. John has already emphasized this test in 2. 7–11; now he returns to emphasize it afresh. The family likeness is bound to appear; the love of the Father will be reproduced in His children. It was so in the earliest days of the human race; here John introduces the one Old Testament reference in his letters, and the only proper name (apart from designations of

Christ or God) in this particular letter.[13] Cain, who murdered his
brother (Gen. 4. 8), showed by that act that he hated him, and his
hatred indicated quite clearly to which spiritual family he belonged.
There is no ground for supposing that Cain is here said to have
been 'of the evil one' (*ek tou ponērou*) in a biological sense, as
though he were the fruit of the tempter's seduction of Eve sexually
understood – an idea current in some Jewish circles around this
time.[14] The statement that 'Cain was of the evil one' is to be
understood in the same sense as our Lord's words to those who
were trying to encompass His death: 'You are of (*ek*) your father
the devil' (John 8. 44). He said so because, in seeking His life,
they showed themselves to be spiritual children of him who 'was
a murderer from the beginning'. In the same way Cain, the first
murderer, showed his spiritual lineage. The verb used here for
'murder' (Gr. *sphazō*) is not found in the New Testament (apart
from this verse) outside Revelation, where it is used of the
slaughtered Lamb (5. 6, 9, 12; 13. 8), of the holy martyrs (6. 9;
18. 24), of the internecine slaughter of war (6. 4) and of the
beast's head that was 'wounded' to death (13. 3). It is a forceful
and vivid word, perhaps used here to bring out the malice afore-
thought with which Abel was murdered; but the fact that its
primary meaning is to cut the throat (as in slaughtering an animal)
hardly justifies K. S. Wuest's translation of it here as 'killed his
brother by severing his jugular vein'![15]

The reason for Cain's hatred, as stated here, is completely in
line with the Genesis narrative; it was 'because his works were
evil, but his brother's were righteous'. When Cain was angry
because his sacrifice was disregarded, God said to him: 'If you do
well, will you not be accepted?' (Gen. 4. 7). He was invited, in
other words, to learn the lesson that comes to such frequent
expression elsewhere in the Old Testament, that 'the sacrifice of
the wicked is an abomination to the LORD, but the prayer of the
upright is his delight' (Prov. 15. 8). Abel, on the other hand,
'received approval as righteous, God bearing witness by accepting
his gifts' (Heb. 11. 4).

The principle of the hostility of the wicked to the righteous is one which John sees operating in the environment of himself and his readers; hence he adds a word of encouragement:

V. 13 Marvel not, brethren, if the world hateth you.

This is a direct echo of the words of our Lord in the upper room: 'If the world hates you, know that it hated me before it hated you. If you were of the world, the world would love its own; but because you are not of the world, but I chose you out of the world, therefore the world hates you. Remember the word that I said to you, "A servant is not greater than his master" ' (John 15. 18–20). The Synoptic record is to the same effect: 'He who hears you hears me', says Jesus to the seventy, 'and he who rejects you rejects me, and he who rejects me rejects him who sent me' (Luke 10. 16), while He reminds the twelve that 'a disciple is not above his teacher, nor a servant above his master; it is enough for the disciple to be like his teacher, and the servant like his master' (Matt. 10. 24, 25).[16]

The world, orientated against God, is, as John has indicated already (1 John 2. 15–17), inherently inimical to the cause of God. Manifestations of its hostility, therefore, should not take the children of God by surprise. The warfare between the two sides continues, although the decisive victory has been won; this gives the children of God confidence that they can overcome the world by faith in Him who has already overcome it (1 John 4. 4; 5. 4 f.; cf. John 16. 33).

V. 14 We know that we have passed out of death into life, because we love the brethren. He that loveth not abideth in death. v. 15 Whosoever hateth his brother is a murderer: and ye know that no murderer hath eternal life abiding in him.

As the presence of murderous hatred is a token that one does not belong to the family of God, the presence of brotherly love is a sure sign that one does belong to it, that one has, through the new birth, 'passed out of death into life' (cf. John 5. 24). The

pronoun 'we' in 'we know' is emphatic – *we*, in contrast to the world
and all who bear the mark of Cain. The definite article before
'brethren' is equivalent, in the context, to an unemphatic possessive
pronoun (cf. NEB: 'we love our brothers'). Love is the supreme
manifestation of the new life, so much so that any one who fails
to manifest it shows that he has never entered into the new life;
he 'abides in death'. 'By this', said Jesus, 'all men will know that
you are my disciples, if you have love for one another' (John 13.
35). These words were spoken immediately after the departure of
Judas, who by his lack of love was self-excluded from the number
of those who were disciples indeed. As with Cain, hatred is the
root which, if unchecked, yields the fruit of murder. Hence our
Lord's warning in the Sermon on the Mount that not just the man
who commits murder, but 'every one who is angry with his brother[17]
shall be liable to judgment' (Matt. 5. 22). If murder, the end-
product of hatred, proves that eternal life is absent, so does the
root principle of hatred itself.

**V. 16   Hereby know we love, because he laid down his
life for us: and we ought to lay down our lives for the brethren.**

When John speaks of love (*agapē*), it is no sentimental emotion
that he has in mind, but something intensely practical. Christians
have one supreme example of love, the love shown by their Lord
in that *He* (as before, John uses the emphatic pronoun *ekeinos*)
'laid down his life' for them. No Christian should speak readily of
his love for others unless he is prepared, if need be, to show that
love as Christ showed His, by giving up his life for them – indeed,
by regarding it as his plain duty so to do. This is what is meant by
showing the love of Christ in one's life.

**V. 17   But whoso hath the world's goods, and beholdeth
his brother in need, and shutteth up his compassion from
him, how doth the love of God abide in him? v. 18 *My* little
children, let us not love in word, neither with the tongue;
but in deed and truth.**

Frequently, however, a Christian will not be called upon to give his life, or even risk it, for his fellows. But he will have frequent opportunity of showing them his love in less exacting ways. Many of them suffer material hardship and privation; a Christian who is blessed with this world's goods will instinctively show 'the love of God'[18] by sharing what he has with others less fortunate.[19] If, on the contrary, he hardens his heart and refuses to show them compassion in such a practical way, what is the use of his talking about 'the love of God'? By paying it lip-service without exhibiting it in kindly and helpful action, he is simply bringing on himself and his associates the charge of hypocrisy. It is love 'in deed and truth' that is expected from a child of God, not the kind of pious talk that devalues the currency of heavenly love because it is unmatched by corresponding action. James says something very much to the same effect: 'If a brother or sister is ill-clad and in lack of daily food, and one of you says to them, "Go in peace, be warmed and filled", without giving them the things needed for the body, what does it profit?' (Jas. 2. 15 f.).

(c) Christian confidence (3. 19–24)

V. 19 **Hereby shall we know that we are of the truth, and shall [1]assure our heart before him, v. 20 whereinsoever our heart condemn us; because God is greater than our heart, and knoweth all things.**

[1] Gr. *persuade*.

The RV rendering of this sentence is followed by RSV: 'By this we shall know that we are of the truth, and reassure our hearts before him whenever our hearts condemn us; for God is greater than our hearts, and he knows everything' (cf. the former of two alternative renderings in NEB margin: ' . . . and reassure ourselves in his sight in matters where our conscience condemns us, because God is greater than our conscience . . .').[20] This involves taking *ho ti* (with which verse 20 begins) not as the conjunction *hoti* 'that' (translated 'for' in AV),[21] but as the neuter of the relative pronoun *hostis*, made indefinite by the addition of *ean* (lit. 'if'), and treated as an accusative of respect: 'in respect of whatsoever'. If we regard the first word of verse 20 as *hoti*, 'that', we find ourselves faced with an unnecessary repetition of the same conjunction at the beginning of the next clause ('that if our heart condemns us, that God is greater than our heart'). NEB text recognizes just such a repetition, and ignores one of the two occurrences of *hoti* in its rendering: 'This is how we may know that we belong to the realm of truth, and convince ourselves in his sight that even if our conscience condemns us, God is greater than our conscience and knows all'. 'The greatness of God, which is above both accusation and Satan, to whom all accusations go back (cf. 1 John 4. 4), consists in the forgiveness which remits guilt and in the power which gives fulfilment of the commandments.'[22]

John has urged his readers to see to it that their love is exercised not in word only but 'in deed and truth'. Such spontaneous, practical and outgoing love is a token that one belongs to the divine fellowship, to the realm of truth (cf. John 18. 37). When we are thus united to the all-knowing God in the bond of love, 'that fact assures us of His sovereign mercy',[23] no matter how hostile a verdict our own conscience may pass upon us. John repeats in effect here with regard to those who dwell in love what he has said earlier about the availability of cleansing for those who walk in the light (1 John 1. 7). The realm of light and the realm of love are one and the same realm, the realm in which the children of God are united in Christ to their heavenly Father.

V. 21   Beloved, if our heart condemn us not, we have boldness toward God; v. 22 and whatsoever we ask, we receive of him, because we keep his commandments, and do the things that are pleasing in his sight.

When God, who is greater than our conscience and pronounces a more authoritative verdict, one based on perfect knowledge of us and of all the relevant circumstances, assures us of the forgiveness of our sins for Christ's sake, we enjoy peace of conscience. The accusation of conscience must always be treated seriously;

only when it is overruled by the pardoning edict of God can its voice be properly hushed. The cleansing from every sin which the blood of Jesus' self-offering procures for us is, as the writer to the Hebrews insists, a cleansing of the *conscience* (Heb. 9. 9, 14; 10. 2, 22).[24] A sin-stained conscience is the most effective barrier between man and God; where the stain is blotted out, the barrier is removed, and instead of separation from God there is 'boldness toward God' – openness in His presence. The writer to the Hebrews, in terms of his special interest, speaks of 'confidence to enter the sanctuary by the blood of Jesus' (Heb. 10. 19). John who has already spoken of the believer's 'boldness' or 'confidence' (*parrhēsia*, lit. 'freedom of speech') in an eschatological sense, of the believer's attitude to Christ at His advent (2. 28; cf. 4. 17), uses it here in a sense not unrelated to its earlier occurrence:

> for the Christian the judgement is not only future, but present; love towards the brethren is the test for abiding in the love of Christ. If we have not a bad conscience in that respect...because we love in deed and truth, we have 'freedom of speech' towards God and may ask Him everything...This is again stressed in 5. 14...This free intercourse with God, which His children abiding in Christ enjoy, has an immediate practical consequence. It has its foundation in Christ, is here now, and will be in the final judgement: 'freedom of speech' in the children of God who are in His love and show forth love.[25]

In the Father's realm of love and light, the children gladly do His bidding and act so as to please Him: they do not find Him difficult to please nor are His commands burdensome to them (cf. 5. 3). It has not occurred to them that there could be any tension between love and obedience; they have learned their Master's lesson: 'If you keep my commandments, you will abide in my love, just as I have kept my Father's commandments and abide in his love' (John 15. 10). In such an atmosphere of love, confidence and obedience it is the most natural thing in the world for the children to 'ask' their Father for what they need, assured that He will give them what they ask. This too forms a part of their Master's teaching: 'if you ask anything of the Father, he will give it to you in my name' (John 16. 23).

V. 23 And this is his commandment, that we should ¹believe in the name of his Son Jesus Christ, and love one another, even as he gave us commandment.

¹ Gr. *believe the name.*

The Father's commandment is the commandment of faith and love. Here the faith is the initial act of believing which leads to the life of faith; this is suggested by the use of the aorist tense (*pisteusōmen*) which is here best regarded as the 'ingressive' aorist. Here the construction following the verb 'believe' is not *eis* ('into') with the accusative (used later in 5. 10, 13)[26] but the simple dative; it is difficult to see a material distinction between the two constructions. The 'name', as so often in biblical literature, is not merely the label of identification attached to the person but the person's character and indeed the person himself. Faith in Christ, then, is the first step of life in the family of God, and this life is a life of love as well as a life of faith. The 'commandment' to 'love one another' has already been emphasized as the commandment which is both new and old (2. 7, 8), the commandment given by Christ to the disciples in the upper room (John 13. 34; 15. 12).

V. 24 And he that keepeth his commandments abideth in him, and he in him. And hereby we know that he abideth in us, by the Spirit which he gave us.

Obedience to the Lord's commandments is not the cause but the proof of His people's dwelling in Him. Moreover, their 'abiding' in Him has as its correlative His 'abiding' in them (cf. John 6. 56). It is by His Spirit that He 'abides' in them, and it is equally by His Spirit that they learn of His 'abiding' in them. This is the first mention of the Spirit in this letter;[27] He appears again as the Spirit of truth in ch. 4 and as the Spirit of witness (as here) in ch. 5. Whether He who 'abides' in us and has given us His Spirit is the Father or the Son (cf. John 15. 4a) is not altogether clear; but in the light of the foregoing clauses (and especially the words 'his Son Jesus Christ' in verse 23) the Father is most probably meant (as explicitly in 4. 12, 15, 16). In fact, however, the Father and the Son together make their home with the believer (John 14. 23) and bestow the gift of the Spirit (in John 14. 26 the Father sends Him in the Son's name; in John 15. 26 the Son sends Him from the Father).

NOTES

1. *Ethics of the Fathers (Pirqe Aboth)* 3. 18.
2. Cf. W. Michaelis in *TDNT* v (Grand Rapids, 1968), p. 366 (*s.v. ὁράω*).
3. Cf. John 15. 18–20 and Synoptic parallels quoted in the comment on 3. 13 (p. 95).
4. Cf. W. Michaelis in *TDNT* v (Grand Rapids, 1968), p. 366 (*s.v. ὁράω*).
5. NEB 'everyone who has this hope before him' is even more open to criticism than AV.
6. 1 John 3. 7; 4. 17.
7. W. Kelly, *The Epistles to the Thessalonians*³ (London, 1953), p. 150 (on 2 Thess. 2. 7).
8. See note on 2. 6 (p. 52).
9. As in Isa. 53. 12, LXX.
10. Here the 'beginning' is the beginning of creation or the beginning of the Bible story.
11. For this use of seed J. C. O'Neill compares 1 Enoch 84. 6, 'establish the flesh of uprightness as a plant of the eternal seed' (*The Puzzle of 1 John*, London, 1966, p. 37). It is possible that John is countering an esoteric use of the concept 'divine seed' among the false teachers, such as we find in the second century among the Valentinians and Naassenes (cf. Irenaeus, *Against Heresies* ii. 19).
12. Cf. Luke 10. 25 ff.
13. It is difficult to find evidence for supposing that here or in Jude 11 there is a covert allusion to predecessors of those second-century Gnostics called Cainites, closely associated with the Naassenes or Ophites (cf. Irenaeus, *Against Heresies* i. 31).
14. The earliest allusion to it is probably in 4 Maccabees (an Alexandrian Jewish document of the first century BC), where the mother of the seven martyred brothers, after referring to the formation of Eve, says 'nor did the false beguiling serpent sully the purity of my maidenhood' (18. 8).
15. *Expanded Translation of the New Testament*, iii (Pickering and Inglis, 1959), p. 198.
16. Cf. Matt. 10. 22a; 24. 9: 'you will be hated by all (nations) for my name's sake'. See also verse 1b above (p. 85).
17. The attempt in later editions of the text to ease this 'hard saying' by the addition of 'without a cause' (cf. AV) is not supported by our earliest authorities.
18. The 'love of God' may be taken here either as our love for God (objective genitive) or God's love for man (subjective genitive). In favour of the former is such a parallel passage as 1 John 4. 20, where love for one's brother is the visible expression of one's love for God (see pp. 114 f.). At the same time such love for one's brother is a reflection of God's own love poured into His children's hearts (cf. Rom. 5. 5). So, in the upper room, Jesus tells His

disciples, 'As the Father has loved me, so have I loved you' (John 15. 9), and charges them 'even as I have loved you, that you also love one another' (John 13. 34).

19. The verb translated 'beholdeth' (RV) is Gr. *theōreō*, which John uses in preference to the present tense of *horaō* (never found in his Gospel or Epistles).

20. The second of the two alternative marginal renderings in NEB is: 'and yet we shall do well to convince ourselves that even if our own conscience condemns us, still more will God who is greater than conscience (condemn us)'. This is a possible way of taking the words by themselves, but is inconsistent with the context.

21. The conjunction *hoti* may mean either 'that' (introducing an indirect statement after a verb of saying or knowing) or 'because' (introducing a causal clause); AV takes it the latter way and translates it 'for'. The distinction in spelling between the conjunction *hoti* (as one word) and the pronoun *ho ti* (as two words) is merely a convention in printing, but a convenient one.

22. W. Grundmann, in *TDNT* iv (Grand Rapids, 1967), p. 538 (*s.v. μέγας*). In appropriate contexts the verb *peithō*, 'persuade' (here translated 'assure' in RV text), has the sense 'conciliate, pacify, set at ease *or* rest', so that peace of conscience in the sight of God appears to be in view here (cf. W. Bauer, W. F. Arndt, F. W. Gingrich, *Greek-English Lexicon of the NT* . . . , Cambridge, 1957, p. 645).

23. B. F. Westcott, *The Epistles of St. John*, p. 117. Westcott's whole comment on these two verses will repay careful study.

24. See comments on 1 John 1. 7 (pp. 43 f.); 2. 2 (pp. 49 f.).

25. W. C. van Unnik, 'The Christian's Freedom of Speech in the NT', *BJRL* 44 (1961–62), p. 486.

26. The construction *pisteuō eis* is the characteristic expression for 'believing in' in the Fourth Gospel, e.g. John 1. 12 ('who believed in his name'), 2. 11 ('his disciples believed in him'), etc.

27. That is to say, the first *explicit* mention; the Spirit is, of course, the 'Holy One' who imparts the 'anointing' of 2. 20, 27 (pp. 70 ff.).

CHAPTER IV

6 THE TWO SPIRITS (4. 1–6)

V. 1 Beloved, believe not every spirit, but prove the spirits, whether they are of God: because many false prophets are gone out into the world.

In the apostolic churches, as in ancient Israel, communications were made from time to time by 'prophets', men and women who spoke as the mouthpieces of a power beyond themselves. Every prophet claimed to be a spokesman of God, to be inspired by the Spirit of truth, but in Old and New Testament times alike it was necessary to test these claims. In Elijah's day we meet prophets of Baal and prophets of Asherah, spokesmen of Canaanite divinities (1 Kings 18. 19), as well as those who, like Elijah himself, were prophets of the God of Israel (1 Kings 18. 4, 13, 22). To distinguish between the former and the latter was no difficult task. It was different when contradictory utterances were made by men claiming to be prophets of the God of Israel. How could it be known for sure that Micaiah the son of Imlah was speaking the truth when he foretold catastrophe at Ramoth-gilead, as against Zedekiah the son of Chenaanah and his companions who so confidently predicted victory? True, the fact that the latter all told King Ahab so unanimously what he wanted to hear was suspicious in itself, and Micaiah had no doubt of the authenticity of his message of doom, having heard it pronounced in the heavenly council;[1] but his ultimate appeal could only be to the event: 'If you return in peace, the LORD has not spoken by me' (1 Kings 22. 28).

Jeremiah in his day stood almost alone as a messenger of doom, opposed by others who prophesied smooth things to the king and people in Jerusalem. How was it to be known whether he or they were right? 'In truth the LORD sent me to you to speak all these words in your ears', said Jeremiah (Jer. 26. 15), but if his hearers refused to accept his assurance, he could only appeal to the out-

come: 'As for the prophet who prophesies peace, when the word
of that prophet comes to pass, then it will be known that the LORD
has truly sent the prophet' (Jer. 28. 9). And in the event Jeremiah
was all too terribly proved to be the true prophet, and the others
to be false prophets.

In Deuteronomy two tests are laid down to determine whether
a prophet is truly a spokesman of God or not: (i) 'if the word does
not come to pass or come true, that is a word which the LORD has
not spoken; the prophet has spoken it presumptuously, you need
not be afraid of him' (Deut. 18. 22); (ii) even if the word which
the prophet speaks comes true, yet if he tries to lead his hearers
astray to serve other gods, he is a false prophet (Deut. 13. 1–5).

The presence of true prophets in the church of New Testament
days stimulated the activity of others who claimed to be prophets
but whose claims were unfounded – or, if they did speak by
inspiration, showed by the content of their utterances that the
spirit that spoke through them was not the Spirit of God. In
either case they were false prophets: men who falsely claimed to
speak by inspiration or men who were inspired by a spirit of
falsehood. To test the prophets then was in effect to test the
spirits by whose impulsion they spoke. John indeed envisages but
two spirits – the Spirit of God and the spirit of Antichrist. In this
he shows a striking affinity with a passage in the Qumran literature
which declares that God 'has appointed for man two spirits in
which to walk until the time of His visitation: the spirits of truth
and falsehood'.[2]

**V. 2 Hereby know ye the Spirit of God: every spirit
which confesseth that Jesus Christ is come in the flesh is of
God: v. 3 and every spirit which [1]confesseth not Jesus is not
of God: and this is the *spirit* of the antichrist, whereof ye have
heard that it cometh; and now it is in the world already.**

[1] Some ancient authorities read *annulleth Jesus.*

A few decades earlier Paul, writing to the Corinthian Christians
on the subject of prophetic utterances, laid down a simple criterion

by which true and false utterances might be distinguished. It was this: what testimony did any such utterance bear to Christ? 'No one speaking by the Spirit of God ever says "Jesus be cursed!" and no one can say "Jesus is Lord" except by the Holy Spirit' (1 Cor. 12. 3). John adopts essentially the same criterion, but rewords it with special reference to the Docetic denial of the Incarnation that was current when he wrote. Test the prophets: ask them if Jesus Christ has come in flesh or not. If they say Yes, then they are to be recognized as speaking by the Spirit of God; if not, then it is not the Spirit of God but the spirit of Antichrist that speaks through them. The words 'every spirit which confesseth not Jesus' could have a wider application than to a denial of His incarnation, although it is evidently this that John has primarily in mind. The variant reading 'annulleth Jesus'[3] may imply the severance of Jesus of Nazareth from the Christ or the Son of God, after the manner of Cerinthus (so R. A. Knox: 'no spirit which would disunite Jesus comes from God'), or it may denote a positive abjuration of His authority, like 'Jesus be cursed!' in 1 Cor. 12. 3. So O. A. Piper argues: 'The phrase *lyei ton Iēsoun*, as its contrast with 1 John 4. 2 and the parallel in 1 Cor. 12. 3 (*anathema Iēsous*) show, signifies a curse, whereby it is believed that Jesus will be deprived of his supernatural power'.[4] Such a denial has already (1 John 2. 18, 22) been branded as a sure sign of Antichrist: the spirit of the great Antichrist of the end-time is already present and operative through these 'many antichrists' who refuse to acknowledge Jesus. No matter how charming, how plausible, how eloquent the prophets in question may be, the test of their witness to Christ and His truth is the test by which they must be judged.

V. 4 **Ye are of God,** *my* **little children, and have overcome them: because greater is he that is in you than he that is in the world.**

John's readers were not more learned, more skilled in philosophical debate, than the false teachers; yet by refusing to be persuaded by the false teachers they had overcome them. This they were able to do because of the indwelling Holy Spirit, whose anointing had imparted to them the true knowledge – a 'built-in spiritual instinct', as it was called in the comment on 1 John 2. 20, enabling them to hold fast to truth and reject error. If 'he that is in you' is the Holy Spirit, 'he that is in the world' is the spirit of falsehood, called 'the spirit of antichrist' in verse 3 and 'the spirit of error' in verse 6.[5]

V. 5 They are of the world: therefore speak they *as* of the world, and the world heareth them. v. 6 We are of God: he that knoweth God heareth us; he who is not of God heareth us not. By this we know the spirit of truth, and the spirit of error.

But why should the leaders of the other party, with their followers, be said to be 'of the world'? Because the philosophy to which they endeavour to accommodate the gospel, depriving it of what makes it the gospel in the process, is current secular philosophy, the prevalent climate of opinion. We have already seen that there is no form of 'worldliness' so inimical to Christianity as this kind of 're-statement'. Such a re-statement is congenial to 'the world' because it is in line with contemporary fashion; nevertheless it is doomed to pass away because with a change in fashion it loses its appeal, which the gospel never does. The gospel, like its faithful preachers, is 'of God', and the people of God recognize it as such through the inward witness of the Spirit in their hearts (cf. 5. 7–11). They are thus in no danger of confusing 'the Spirit of truth' with 'the spirit of error', the spirit that leads men astray (cf. 2. 26).

7 Walking in Love (4. 7–21)

(a) In praise of love (4. 7–12)

Like Paul in 1 Corinthians 13, John in this section has his hymn in praise of heavenly love.

V. 7 Beloved, let us love one another: for love is of God; and every one that loveth is begotten of God, and knoweth

God. v. 8 **He that loveth not knoweth not God; for God is
love.**

The love of which John, like Paul, speaks is self-giving love, not
acquisitive love. It is sometimes suggested that the verb *agapaō* and
the noun *agapē*, which are used here as so commonly in the New
Testament, bear the former sense intrinsically as against *erōs*,
which denotes possessive love; this is the implication of the title
of Anders Nygren's great work *Agape and Eros*.[6] But it is not
a question of the intrinsic sense of the words used (in the
Septuagint of 2 Sam. 13. 1–15 both *agapē* and *agapaō* are used
of Amnon's passion for Tamar) but of the sense placed on
them by speakers or writers. The love which the New Testament
enjoins involves a consuming passion for the well-being of others,
and this love has its wellspring in God. Since 'love is of God', says
John, 'let us love one another'; the children of God must reproduce
their Father's nature. Those who show such love to one another
give proof in doing so that they are God's children and that it is
they (not those who say so much about the true *gnōsis* or knowledge
of God without regard for the love of God) who really know Him.
Those, on the other hand, from whose lives such love is absent
give proof by that fact that they have never begun to know God,
however confident their claims may be. To know the God of love
means to manifest His love. 'God is love' is as compressed a
statement of the gospel as is well imaginable; yet it is no more a
reversible statement than is its counterpart in 1 John 1. 5, 'God is
light'. 'Love is of God'; love is divine; but one can no more say
that 'love is God' than one could say that 'light is God'. 'God is
love' is an affirmation about God; while it is a compressed statement of the gospel, it is so in the sense which is spelt out in the
following sentence, 'that God sent his only Son into the world, so
that we might live through him'. It is this act of God that gives
meaning to His love; indeed, it is this act that gives meaning to love
absolutely, in the sense which it bears in the Johannine writings
and in the New Testament generally.

The gospel gives no countenance to the facile and optimistic assertion that God is love as though, in the light of all the facts of life, this were the easiest of all things to believe. Bishop Gore, who is reported to have called it the hardest of all things to believe ('believe that, and you can believe everything else'), speaks of many

> who certainly have 'the will to believe', but who find the belief that God is love very difficult. The days seem to them far off when it was possible with any plausibility to contrast the 'simple doctrine' that God is love with the 'elaborate and difficult dogmas' of the Church. For they feel that it is only the dogmas that Jesus Christ is God, and His mind God's mind, and that God, the God of nature, really vindicated Him by raising Him from the dead, that do in fact sustain their tottering faith and hope in God.[7]

The Christian affirmation that God is love is not sustained by ignoring the cross, in all its stark obscenity, but by setting it in the forefront of the situation.

V. 9 Herein was the love of God manifested [1]in us, that God hath sent his only begotten Son into the world, that we might live through him. v. 10 Herein is love, not that we loved God, but that he loved us, and sent his Son *to be* the propitiation for our sins.

[1] Or, *in our case.*

John has already pointed to Christ's laying down His life for His people as the perfect manifestation of love (3. 16). He returns to the sacrifice of Christ again, and presents it from the Father's point of view, in words similar to those of the Gospel (John 3. 16). The supreme act of God's love was His sending 'his only begotten Son into the world'. As in the Gospel, the adjective 'only be-gotten' (*monogenēs*) is used in a sense which combines the ideas of 'only-begotten' and 'well-loved' (like Heb. *yachid* in Gen. 22. 2, which is rendered *agapētos*, 'beloved', in the Septuagint, but *monogenēs* in Josephus, Aquila and Heb. 11. 17).[8] The purpose of His thus sending His Son is our blessing – 'that we should receive life through him', for thus the ingressive force of the aorist *zēsōmen* may be expressed. Here the initiative lies entirely with God; before there was any possibility of our exercising such love

He first manifested it when He 'loved us and sent his Son as a propitiation for our sins'. These last words are repeated from 2. 2, wherein the meaning of 'propitiation' (*hilasmos*) has been discussed.[9]

V. 11 **Beloved, if God so loved us, we also ought to love one another. v. 12 No man hath beheld God at any time: if we love one another, God abideth in us, and his love is perfected in us:**

God's love for us, then, supplies the motive power for His people's love for one another. The adverb 'so' (Gr. *houtōs*) has the emphatic force here that it has at the beginning of John 3. 16. 'We also ought to love one another', because we are His children. If the children of God must be holy because He is holy (Lev. 11. 44 f.; 1 Pet. 1. 15 f.) and merciful because He is merciful (Luke 6. 36), so they must be loving because He is loving – not with the 'must' of external compulsion but with the 'must' of inward constraint: God's love is poured into their hearts by the Holy Spirit whom they have received (Rom. 5. 5). They are, in fact, the witnesses on earth to God's love. 'No one has ever beheld God', but He may be seen in His children when they love one another. John has already made this statement (except for the variant 'seen', *heōraken*, instead of 'beheld', *tetheatai*) in the prologue to his Gospel, but there the invisible God has been made known on earth by His Son (John 1. 18). Now that the Son has returned to the Father, God is made known on earth by those who through faith in His Son have become His children – if they love one another. The love of God displayed in His people is the strongest apologetic that God has in the world. When His love is planted in their hearts, and He Himself thus dwells within them, His love is 'perfected' in the complementary response which it finds in them, towards Him and towards their fellows. It is in this way that they are not only holy and merciful as He is holy and merciful, but, as enjoined by their Lord in the Matthaean version of the Sermon on the Mount, 'perfect' as their 'heavenly Father is perfect' (Matt. 5. 48), and all through that

perfection of love poured out for them in the sacrifice of the cross.
'The only kind of personal union . . . with which we are acquainted',
says C. H. Dodd, 'is love'. John, he continues:

> makes use of the strongest expressions for union with God that con-
> temporary religious language provided, in order to assure his readers
> that he does seriously mean what he says: that through faith in
> Christ we may enter into a personal community of life with the
> eternal God, which has the character of *agapē*, which is essentially
> supernatural and not of this world, and yet plants its feet firmly in
> this world, not only because real *agapē* cannot but express itself in
> practical conduct, but also because the crucial act of *agapē* was
> actually performed in history, on an April day about AD 30, at a
> supper-table in Jerusalem, in a garden across the Kidron valley, in the
> headquarters of Pontius Pilate, and on a Roman cross at Golgotha.
> So concrete, so actual, is the nature of the divine *agapē*; yet none the
> less for that, by entering into the relation of *agapē* thus opened up for
> men, we may dwell in God and He in us.[10]

(b) Perfect love and sound doctrine (4. 13–21)

**V. 13   hereby know we that we abide in him, and he in
us, because he hath given us of his Spirit. v. 14 And we have
beheld and bear witness that the Father hath sent the Son
to be the Saviour of the world.**

Not only is God's love poured into His children's hearts through
the Holy Spirit; an appreciation of God's truth has been imparted
to them by the same Spirit. The Spirit of love is the Spirit of truth.
The Spirit persuades and enables us to believe in Jesus as the Son
of God; He communicates to us the new life which is ours as
members of God's regenerate family; it is through Him that we
remain in union with the ever-living Christ and He with us; it is
through His inward witness that we receive the power to bear our
witness in turn. Thus our Lord's promise in the upper room is
fulfilled: 'when the Counsellor comes, whom I shall send to you
from the Father, even the Spirit of truth, who proceeds from the
Father, he will bear witness to me; and you also are witnesses,
because you have been with me from the beginning' (John 15. 26,
27). While these words were primarily applicable to His com-

panions in His earthly ministry, they have become applicable to
later generations of disciples also who have heard the testimony of
the eyewitnesses and having thus had fellowship with them have
fellowship also with the Father and with His Son Jesus Christ
(1 John 1. 3). The substance of the witness of the Spirit and of
those whom He indwells is this: 'the Father has sent the Son as
Saviour of the world'. Here is another summary of the gospel,
expressed this time not in the form of a permanently valid proposition, like 'God is love', but in the form of a historical statement
in the light of which the validity of the proposition is seen. The
designation 'the Saviour of the world' is peculiar to the Johannine
writings in the New Testament; in addition to its single occurrence
in the First Epistle it occurs once in the Gospel (John 4. 42), on the
lips (significantly enough) of Samaritans, who had no interest in
promises which were attached to the tribe of Judah but great
interest in promises which spoke of a world-wide salvation. As
earlier, where he speaks of Christ as 'the propitiation . . . for all the
world' (1 John 2. 2), so here John ascribes the widest scope to the
saving purpose of God. The pronoun 'we' in 'we have beheld' is
emphatic;[11] John may be thinking in the first instance of himself
and his original associates, who delivered to others the testimony of
what they had 'beheld' (cf. 1 John 1. 1) so that others in turn might
bear the same testimony; but in the light of verse 16, where the
similarly emphatic 'we' can scarcely have this force, he more
probably thinks of himself and his readers, by contrast with those
who had left the fellowship, thus renouncing the bond of love and
the witness of the Spirit. This appears to be confirmed by the words
which immediately follow.

V. 15 **Whosoever shall confess that Jesus is the Son of God, God abideth in him, and he in God.**

John has just said that if we love one another, God abides in us
(verse 12); now he says that God abides in us if we 'confess that
Jesus is the Son of God'. He seems to be conscious of no tension
at all between Christian love and Christian truth. The love of God

was manifested in the giving up of His Son; if Jesus is not the Son of God and if His death does not atone for the sins of men, then there is no Christian message and Christian love and truth fall together, as they stand together if that message is true. If none can acknowledge Jesus as the Son of God apart from the enlightenment and empowering of the Spirit, it is equally true that the mutual coinherence of God and His children is the Spirit's work, as is also the outflowing of the love of God through them to others. Mutual indwelling, perfect love and confession of the truth are bound up in one another; God has joined them together and they may not be put asunder.

V. 16 And we know and have believed the love which God hath ¹in us. God is love; and he that abideth in love abideth in God, and God abideth in him.

¹ Or, *in our case.*

What is here being said about love is no matter of mere theory; it is something which is proved in experience and faith. In speaking of 'the love which God has in us'¹² John may mean more than His love *for* us; that is included, indeed, but the love which God has for His children is poured into their hearts by His Spirit and flows out to others. The love which dwells in the community of God's children and which they show one to another is His love imparted to them. More than that: the God of love imparts Himself to His people, so dwelling within them that they, in their turn, dwell in His love and dwell in Him (cf. verse 12).

V. 17 Herein is love made perfect with us, that we may have boldness in the day of judgement; because as he is, even so are we in this world. v. 18 There is no fear in love: but perfect love casteth out fear, because fear hath punishment; and he that feareth is not made perfect in love.

The perfection of love, John has already said (verse 12), is realized when God dwells in His children and they love another. This perfection of love, he adds here, is specially manifested in the confidence with which they will face the day of judgment.[13] This is the advent day of 2. 28, where those who dwell in God are assured that they will have no need to shrink from His presence with shame on that great day. Christian confidence and Christian love go together; they find their antithesis in shame and fear. A sense of awe in face of the majesty and righteousness of God is proper; anything in the nature of unnerving fear at the coming of Him whose name is love denies the love 'which God has in us'. Here we have the last occurrence of the phrase *kathōs ekeinos*, 'as He', in reference to the risen Christ: 'as he is, so even are we in this world'. It was this revelation that replaced fear by confidence in John Bunyan's heart when the words of Rom. 3. 24, 'justified freely by his grace, through the redemption that is in Christ Jesus', were expounded to him thus as though by a voice from heaven:

> Sinner, thou thinkest that because of thy sins and infirmities I cannot save thy soul, but behold my Son is by me, and upon him I look, and not on thee, and will deal with thee according as I am pleased with him.[14]

The day of judgment need have no terror for anyone who has appropriated the assurance of John 5. 24: 'he who hears my word and believes him who sent me, has eternal life; he does not come into judgment, but has passed from death to life'. Nor can it have terror for anyone who knows himself united in faith and love to the Son of Man to whom all judgment has been entrusted by the Father (John 5. 22, 27). All such terror is banished by the 'perfect love' in which the members of God's family live. 'Fear has to do with punishment' (RSV),[15] but 'punishment' (*kolasis*) is the portion of those who through disobedience are 'condemned already', not of those who, believing in the Son of God, are 'not condemned' (John 3. 18). A believer who contemplates the judgment day with trepidation, says John, is one in whom divine love has not yet reached its full maturity, and one therefore who himself has not yet reached full spiritual maturity. Charles Wesley was right when he defined entire sanctification in terms of

> A heart in every thought renewed
> And full of love divine.

**V. 19 We love, because he first loved us. v. 20 If a man
say, I love God, and hateth his brother, he is a liar: for he
that loveth not his brother whom he hath seen, ¹cannot love
God whom he hath not seen. v. 21 And this commandment
have we from him, that he who loveth God love his brother
also.**

¹ Many ancient authorities read *how can he love God whom he hath not seen?*

AV, following the Received Text, reads 'we love him' in verse 19,
but the textual evidence makes it clear that 'him' is a later addition
by scribes or editors who felt that an explicit object was necessary.
(A few other scribes or editors from the same motive added 'God'
as the object.) But in the context 'we love' is the more suitable
reading as it is the better attested one. We love God, it is true, but
in loving Him we inevitably love His children. In taking the
initiative in loving us, He not only showed us how to love one
another (cf. 3. 11) but He imparted the desire and the power to
follow this example of His. Our Lord made it plain that the two
great Old Testament commandments of love to God and love to
one's neighbour are two sides of one coin (Mark 12. 29–31; cf.
Luke 10. 27 f.), and when He said to His disciples in the upper
room, 'If you love me, you will keep my commandments' (John 14.
15), He laid down as His new and chief commandment that they
should love one another as He loved them, so that everyone would
know that they were truly His disciples (John 13. 34 f.). Similarly
in this letter John has already emphasized that brotherly love
characterizes the children of God; to hate one's brother is to proclaim one's kinship with Cain (3. 10–18). Here the same lesson
is emphasized afresh; once more the test of love is applied. Where
God's love or our love for God is mentioned, John makes no distinction between the Father and the Son; alike in loving men and
in being loved by them in return the Son and the Father are one
(cf. John 10. 30). Peter speaks of Christ as the One 'whom, not
having seen', His people love (1 Pet. 1. 8); John agrees, but adds
that love for the unseen One will be attested by love for His

people whom we do see. Much verbal expression of devotion for the person of Christ can co-exist with remarkably un-Christian attitudes towards the people of Christ; John's comment on this inconsistency is sharp and undisguised. In this he is at one with his Master, who declared that in the judgment behaviour towards His brethren will be counted as behaviour towards Himself (Matt. 25. 31–46). Those whose lives are marked by lack of love in this regard may well have a sense of trepidation as they look forward to the day of review.

NOTES

1. Cf. Jer. 23. 18, 22, where the false prophets of Jeremiah's day have no authentic message to deliver because none of them 'has stood in the council of the LORD'; if they had, says God, 'then they would have proclaimed my words to my people, and they would have turned them from their evil way'.
2. *Rule of the Community* 3. 18 f. These two spirits are otherwise called the Prince of Light and the Angel of Darkness (see note on 1 John 1. 5, p. 41).
3. This variant appears in the margin of the important codex 1739, was known to Irenaeus, Clement of Alexandria and Origen, and is attested by the Latin version.
4. 'I John and the Didache of the Primitive Church', *JBL* 66 (1947), pp. 443 f.
5. Cf. Eph. 2. 2: 'the spirit that is now at work in the sons of disobedience'.
6. Translated from Swedish (London, 1932–39).
7. C. Gore, *Belief in God* (Penguin edition, 1939), p. 150.
8. W. Bauer, W. F. Arndt and F. W. Gingrich, *Greek-English Lexicon of the NT* . . . (Cambridge, 1957), mention the further possible meaning 'begotten of the Only One' (*s.v. μονογενής*).
9. See p. 50.
10. C. H. Dodd, *The Interpretation of the Fourth Gospel* (Cambridge, 1953), pp. 199 f.
11. Gr. *hēmeis*, as in 3. 14, 16; 4. 6, 10, 11, 16, 17, 19 (inclusive), and 1. 4 (exclusive).
12. Gr. *en hēmin*, as in verse 9. Cf. the use of *en* in Acts 4. 2; Gal. 1. 16.
13. The RSV rendering 'confidence for the day of judgment' is scarcely adequate; the confidence is maintained when the day of judgment arrives – 'confidence on the day of judgement' (NEB).
14. *Grace Abounding*, §§ 257, 258.
15. Cf. NEB: 'fear brings with it the pains of judgement'. A verbal parallel to this clause is provided by Philo where, speaking of the effects of shame and fear in one who has broken the eighth commandment, he says: 'Fear is a sign that he considers himself worthy of punishment (*kolasis*), because it is punishments (*kolaseis*) that (in prospect) instil fear' (*Special Laws* iv. 6).

CHAPTER V

8 THE VICTORY OF FAITH (5. 1–5)

V. 1 Whosoever believeth that Jesus is the Christ is begotten of God: and whosoever loveth him that begat loveth him also that is begotten of him.

To love the Father (whom we have not seen) involves loving His child (whom we can see): thus John sums up what has just been said. And who is the child of God? Any one who believes that Jesus is the Christ. In the Johannine writings this means more than assenting to the proposition that Jesus is the promised Messiah; it means personal faith in Him, personal union with Him, who has been revealed 'in the flesh' (4. 2) as the Christ and Son of God. In the Gospel it is to all who received the living Word, to all 'who believed in his name', that God 'gave power to become children of God' (John 1. 12); the Gospel in fact was written in order that its readers might 'believe that Jesus is the Christ, the Son of God' and thus 'have life in his name' (John 20. 31).

V. 2 Hereby we know that we love the children of God, when we love God, and do his commandments. v. 3 For this is the love of God, that we keep his commandments:

Love to God and love to His children, love to God and obedience to God, are so completely involved in each other that any one of them implies the other two. A man may say he loves God, but his love to God can become manifest to himself and to others only in so far as he obeys God's commandments and shows practical love to God's children. It is easier to deceive ourselves in these matters than it is to deceive others. If we tell them that 'we love God', they will look for some visible evidence; we should look for some visible evidence ourselves. If the visible evidence is forthcoming, it will not be necessary to say that 'we love God'; the evidence will say so more convincingly. Keeping the commandments of God includes first and foremost keeping the primary commandment of love. 'If love to men proves the truth of our love to God, love to God proves the worth of our love to men'.[1] There is indeed much genuine and practical philanthropy in the world which rests on a humanist basis; John insists that love to man finds its strongest and most enduring motive in love to God in whose image man was made and by whose grace man was redeemed. Again, the test of love and the test of obedience are seen to be not two tests, but one.

V. 3b and his commandments are not grievous. v. 4 For whatsoever is begotten of God overcometh the world: and this is the victory that hath overcome the world, *even* our faith. v. 5 And who is he that overcometh the world, but he that believeth that Jesus is the Son of God?

The punctuation of the clause 'and his commandments are not grievous' (RSV, NEB 'burdensome') is doubtful; it may go more closely with the foregoing or with the following words. The argument for taking them with the following words is that the following words explain why the commandments of God are not burdensome: it is because the new life imparted to members of the family of God carries with it a new desire to do His will and a new power to give effect to that desire. Not only so, this new power enables them to 'overcome the world' – everything that is opposed to God. This may be the world of current thought inimical to the 'teaching of Christ' which was communicated 'from the beginning'; it may be the world with its attractiveness and pretentiousness against which the readers of this letter are put on their guard in 2. 15–17; it may be the world in open hostility, meting out to the disciples of Christ the same kind of treatment as was meted out to their Master. In the Gospel, Jesus' last word to His disciples before His passion is, 'In the world you have tribulation; but be of good cheer, I have overcome the world' (John 16. 33). By their faith in Jesus as the Son of God[2] they are so united with Him that His victory becomes theirs; they conquer by His power. So John has already encouraged his readers: 'You are of God, little children, and you have overcome them, because he who is in you is greater than he who is in the world' (4. 4). In the Revelation, too, every kind of incentive is held out to the hard-pressed disciples to maintain their faith and so prove themselves 'overcomers'. When 'the deceiver of the whole world' launches his final and deadliest attack against them, they win the victory over him with the same weapons as their Master used: 'they have conquered him by the blood of the Lamb and by the word of their testimony, for they loved not their lives even unto death' (Rev. 12. 11). This victory over the world and every other hostile force was common Christian experience in the apostolic age: with the language of the Johannine writings we may compare Paul's assurance that 'in all these things we are more than conquerors through him who loved us' (Rom. 8. 37) and his thanksgiving to God 'who gives us the victory through our Lord Jesus Christ' (1 Cor. 15. 57).

9   THE GROUND OF ASSURANCE (5. 6–12)

V. 6   This is he that came by water and blood, even Jesus Christ; not [1]**with the water only, but** [1]**with the water and** [1]**with the blood.**

[1] Gr. *in.*

We are naturally reminded of the incident in the passion narrative of the Gospel of John, in which blood and water come out from our Lord's side after His dead body is pierced with the soldier's lance (John 19. 34).[3] In the narrative much importance is clearly attached to this phenomenon, emphatically supported as it is by trustworthy eyewitness testimony (John 19. 35): whatever else it may signify, it does (in the Evangelist's intention) signify our Lord's real humanity. Something of the same significance is present here, though the details are to be interpreted rather differently. The sequence 'water and blood' is not accidental, but corresponds to the historical sequence of our Lord's baptism and passion.[4] Cerinthus, we recall, taught that 'the Christ' (a spiritual being) came down on the man Jesus when He was baptized but left Him before He died. The Christ, that is to say, came through *water* (baptism) but not through *blood* (death).⁵ To this misrepresentation of the truth John replies that the One whom believers acknowledge to be the Son of God (verse 5) came 'not with the water only but with the water and with the blood': the One who died on the cross was as truly the Christ, the Son of God, as the One who was baptized in Jordan. This is the primary force of John's words; if there is any substance in the sacramental significance which has been discerned in them (mentioned in the note on verse 8), it is at best secondary.⁶

V. 7 **And it is the Spirit that beareth witness, because the Spirit is the truth.**

John and his associates bear witness to the truth of what they have seen and heard (1. 2; 4. 14), but behind their witness lies the witness of the Spirit (cf. 3. 24; 4. 13). This is completely in line with the promise of our Lord in the Gospel: 'when the Counsellor comes, . . . the Spirit of truth, . . . he will bear witness to me; and you also are witnesses, because you have been with me from the beginning' (John 15. 26 f.). The fulfilment of this promise was realized early in apostolic history: 'we are witnesses to these things', said the apostles to the Sanhedrin when challenged for proclaiming the crucified and risen Jesus; 'and so is the Holy Spirit whom God has given to those who obey him' (Acts 5. 32). The Spirit witnesses in the believer's heart and in the believing community; their experience of His power and guidance confirms the truth of the gospel to which they have committed themselves. To this 'inward witness' must be added the 'outward witness' of the Spirit in Holy Scripture; while this aspect of the Spirit's witness does not come to the fore in this epistle, it is prominent in most of the New Testament documents: the Spirit who spoke through the prophets bore witness by their written words, interpreted in the light of their fulfilment in Christ, to the truth of the message which the apostles proclaimed.⁷ Whatever form the witness of the Spirit takes, it can be implicitly trusted, for 'the Spirit of truth', as He is repeatedly called in the upper room discourse in the Gospel (John 14. 17; 15. 26; 16. 13), is Himself 'the truth'.[8]

V. 8   For there are three who bear witness, the Spirit, and the water, and the blood: and the three agree in one.

It is in the community who hold fast to what they were taught from the beginning, those who believe in Him who came by water and blood, that the Spirit is present to 'bear witness';[9] those who deny the truth conveyed by 'the water and the blood' cannot lay claim to the Spirit who bears witness by means of these. The Spirit's ministry in the world includes as one of its principal elements the bearing of witness to Christ; this He did as early as the baptism, when He descended like a dove and remained on Him (John 1. 32 f.). The Baptist saw and accepted this witness of the Spirit, and thereafter he himself bore witness 'that this is the Son of God' (John 1. 34). Again, when the death of Jesus was certified by means of the soldier's lance-thrust instead of the breaking of His legs, the witness of the Spirit of prophecy was doubly confirmed, as the Evangelist is at pains to underline (John 19. 36 f.), while true witness was further borne by one 'who saw it' (John 19. 35). The witness of the 'water' and the witness of the 'blood' are thus aspects of the Spirit's witness. The witness which all three bear is 'one' and the same:

> His Spirit answers to the blood,
> And tells me I am born of God.

Another account of 'the Spirit and the water and the blood' interprets them in terms of three stages of Christian initiation in certain areas of the early church – (a) the reception of the Spirit (with or without the laying on of hands); (b) baptism; (c) first communion. This sequence is attested for Syria, by contrast with the Christian West. This interpretation has been worked out in particular by Wolfgang Nauck,[10] who finds affinities between this primitive Christian order and the practice of certain Jewish communities, especially the procedure for admission to the covenant-community of Qumran and the procedure reflected by the treatise

Joseph and Aseneth[11] and the *Testament of Levi*.[12] That the mention of 'blood' alone without a companion mention of the body should denote the Eucharist is unlikely, and the context of John's argument implies a historical rather than a sacramental interpretation. The most that can be said is that Christian communities which observed this particular order of initiation (cf. Acts 10. 44 ff. for an apostolic precedent) may have appealed to the sequence of the three witnesses in our present text. There could be an allusion to the witness which the Spirit bears to and through believers as they identify themselves with Christ in baptism and declare their 'interest in the Saviour's blood' in communion, but any such allusion would be secondary to the main thrust of the psssage.

V. 9   If we receive the witness of men, the witness of God is greater: for the witness of God is this, that he hath borne witness concerning his Son. v. 10 He that believeth on the Son of God hath the witness in him: he that believeth not God hath made him a liar; because he hath not believed in the witness that God hath borne concerning his Son.

The witness of the Spirit and the witness of the Father are one: at our Lord's baptism, for example, the Spirit's descent and the Father's voice alike proclaimed Jesus to be the Son of God. This witness that God has 'borne concerning his Son' is amplified in the gospel narratives – we may recall that the Gospels of Mark and John alike, in their respective ways, are concerned to produce within their readers the conviction that Jesus is the Son of God (compare Mark 1. 1; 15. 39 with John 20. 31). Whoever, by accepting 'the witness of God', believes in the Son of God,[13] has the witness in himself:[14] the record is no longer simply something that he has heard from others, or reads in a book; it comes to life in his own experience, because the witness-bearing Spirit now resides within him. On the other hand, refusal to accept 'the witness of God' is tantamount to calling Him a liar (cf. 1. 10). So clearcut is the antithesis which John sees between belief and unbelief.

**V. 11 And the witness is this, that God gave unto us
eternal life, and this life is in his Son. v. 12 He that hath the
Son hath the life; he that hath not the Son of God hath not the
life.**

'Eternal life' (Gr. *zōē aiōnios*) means in the first instance 'the
life of the age to come', the life of the resurrection age. As such, it
is something to be experienced in the future. But in Jesus the
powers of the age to come have manifested themselves already; He
proclaims Himself to be 'the resurrection and the life' in such a
way that those who are united by faith to Him enjoy eternal life
here and now, whereas those who reject Him are 'condemned
already' without waiting for the sentence of the great day (compare
John 11. 25 f. with 3. 18). The Son of God who died and rose
again is the embodiment of 'the eternal life which was with the
Father and was made manifest to us' (1. 2), so that to have 'the
Son' is to have 'the life' and failure to have Him means forfeiture of
'the life'. Very much the same statement is made in the Gospel (cf.
especially John 3. 36); here probably John has in mind more particularly those false teachers, who, by denying that Jesus Christ
had come in the flesh (cf. 4. 2), showed that they had not 'the Son
of God' in the sense in which the apostolic message had proclaimed Him 'from the beginning', and showed by the same token
that they were outside the pale of eternal life.

10 EPILOGUE (5. 13–21)

**V. 13 These things have I written unto you, that ye may
know that ye have eternal life, *even* unto you that believe on
the name of the Son of God.**

Towards the end of the Gospel of John its readers are told that
the 'signs' recorded in it 'are written that you may believe[15] that
Jesus is the Christ, the Son of God, and that believing you may
have life in his name' (John 20. 31). The First Letter is written to
those, who do 'believe in[16] the name of the Son of God' to assure
them that it is they who, in virtue of this belief, possess eternal life.

The question where eternal life was to be found, as has been said above, had probably been the subject of animated debate, the seceders claiming that it was to be found in their circle by reason of the higher teaching which they had embraced. But John affirms that the seceders, by denying the incarnation of the Son of God, did not truly believe in His person (which is what is meant by 'the name' in such contexts as the present) and so had no claim on the eternal life which was to be had in Him alone. While this contemporary situation may have been uppermost in John's mind, however, his affirmation has a wider reference; because of its abiding validity it has remained a classic and effective text conveying the assurance of eternal life in all generations to those who believe in the name of the Son of God.

V. 14   And this is the boldness which we have toward him, that, if we ask anything according to his will, he heareth us: v. 15 and if we know that he heareth us whatsoever we ask, we know that we have the petitions which we have asked of him.

This is the fourth occurrence of 'boldness' or confidence (Gr. *parrhēsia*) in 1 John (cf. 2. 28; 3. 21; 4. 17 for the other occurrences). Here the confidence which is particularly in the writer's mind is related to the free access and freedom of speech which the children of God enjoy as they come to their Father to present their requests to Him. There is a close relation between these words and the promise of Jesus to the disciples in the upper room: 'Whatever you ask in my name, I will do it, that the Father may be glorified in the Son; if you ask anything in my name, I will do it' (John 14. 13 f.; cf. 15. 7, 16; 16. 23 f.). If in the Gospel and the Epistle alike it is not always clear whether the request is made to the Father or to the Son, this is because of the perfect unity subsisting between the Father and the Son. It is through the Son that the children approach the Father; it is in the Son that the Father's grace is conveyed to the children. With this confidence, the children know that the Father's hearing of their prayers is synonymous with His answering their prayers. 'Constantly', said C. H. Spurgeon, 'we hear God addressed as "the hearer *and answerer* of prayer", a mere vulgar and useless pleonasm, for the Scripture idea of God's hearing prayer is just his answering it – "O thou that hearest prayer, unto thee shall all flesh come".'[17]

V. 16 **If any man see his brother sinning a sin not unto death, [1]he shall ask, and** *God* **will give him life for them that sin not unto death. There is [2]a sin unto death: not concerning this do I say that he should make request. v. 17 All un-righteousness is sin: and there is [2]a sin not unto death.**

[1] Or, *he shall ask and shall give him life,* even *to them &c.*   [2] Or, *sin.*

After the general assurance about the answering of prayer in verses 14 and 15 comes this special encouragement to pray for a fellow-Christian in spiritual need. The present participle 'sinning' may denote engagement in a sinful course rather than committing an isolated act of sin; we cannot be sure, and in the one case as in the other the 'brother' could well be regarded as standing in the need of prayer. The question arises what the distinction is between 'sin unto death' and sin which is 'not unto death' (since 'not' represents the Greek negative *mē*, it is implied that the reference is to the kind or class of sin which is 'not unto death'). We should not think of the distinction between venial and mortal sin as this has been traditionally elaborated in moral theology.[18] The distinction is one which John's readers were expected to recognize. But it is difficult to see how they could recognize the distinction except by the result. Elsewhere in the New Testament instances occur of sins which caused the death of the persons committing them, when these persons were church members. Ananias and Sapphira come to mind (Acts 5. 1–11); the incestuous man at Corinth is possibly another example, if he suffered 'the destruction of the flesh' in the literal sense (1. Cor. 5. 5), and those other Corinthian Christians who are said to have 'fallen asleep' because of their profanation of the Lord's Supper (1 Cor. 11. 30) certainly provide further examples. It may be, then, that by 'sin unto death' John means an act or course of sin which has resulted in the death of the sinning brother. If so, his words 'I do not say that one is to pray for that'[19] (RSV) amount to a deprecation of praying for the dead. Another possibility is that he has apostasy in mind.[20] In that case, he does not encourage prayer for the restoration of those who, like the false teachers of 2. 18–23, had manifested the spirit of Antichrist and shown where they properly belonged by quitting the fellowship in which alone eternal life was to be found. With regard to such men John may have felt much as the writer to the Hebrews did in another situation, that it was 'impossible to renew them to repentance';[21] renunciation of the apostolic witness to Christ and His saving power was indeed a 'sin unto death'.

Apart from such an exceptional case (whichever form it took), John gives his readers every encouragement to pray for their fellow-believers whom they see falling into sin. Such prayer is in line with the ministry of their Advocate with the Father. Foreseeing the certainty of Peter's fall, their Lord on the eve of His passion assured that self-confident apostle of His intercession: 'I have prayed for you that your faith may not fail; and when you have turned again, strengthen your brethren' (Luke 22. 32); this too was an example of a service which His disciples could perform for one another, with similar happy effects in those who were thus prayed for. 'All unrighteousness (RSV, NEB: 'all wrongdoing') is sin', but not every unrighteous act is irremediably mortal, if it be repented of; and the intercession of a fellow-Christian may be a most effective means of inducing repentance and reliance on the promise given earlier in this letter: 'If we confess our sins, he is faithful and righteous to forgive us our sins and cleanse us from all unrighteousness' (1 John 1. 9).

V. 18 We know that whosoever is begotten of God sinneth not; but he that was begotten of God keepeth [1]him, and the evil one toucheth him not. v. 19 We know that we are of God, and the whole world lieth in the evil one. v. 20 And we know that the Son of God is come, and hath given us an understanding, that we know him that is true,

[1] Or, *himself.*

As he draws his exhortation to a conclusion, John reminds his readers of some of the basic articles of the faith which they have held 'from the beginning'. He has already told them that their knowledge derives from the anointing they have received from 'the Holy One' (2. 20); now he mentions some of the most important things that they 'know'. It is significant that the first of these underlines the ethical implication of their faith: the child of God does not sin. Earlier in the letter John has said that the child of God does not sin because he abides in God (3. 6, 9); there we saw that he wants to make it quite clear that anyone who leads a life of sin is shown thereby not to belong to the family of God. Here the reason the child of God does not sin is expressed in different terms; it is because the Son of God keeps him, protecting him against the designs of the enemy of souls. The adjective clause 'whosoever is begotten of God' represents a Greek construction with the perfect participle passive *gegennēmenos*, and refers to every child of God; the expression 'he that was begotten of God' represents the construction with the aorist participle passive *gennētheis*, and denotes the one and only Son of God, as RSV indicates by (exceptionally) capitalizing the antecedent pronoun 'He'. (NEB makes the meaning equally clear by rendering more freely, 'We know that no child of God is a sinner; it is the Son of God who keeps him safe, and the evil one cannot touch him'.[22]) The Received Text obscures the sense by reading 'himself' (Gr. *heauton* or *hauton*) after 'keepeth' instead of 'him' (*auton*); hence the misleading rendering of AV, 'he that is begotten of God keepeth himself', as though the subject of 'keepeth' were the child of God (as at the beginning of the verse) and not (as in fact it is) the Son of God.

The second thing that 'we know' is more personal: 'we know that we are of God'; and the basis of this knowledge can only be that the tests of eternal life have been applied and the results have been positive. To claim to belong to the family of God is one thing; to exhibit the marks of His family, in the light of the criteria of obedience, love and perseverance, is another thing. In the case of John and his 'little children', these criteria have been satisfied. As for those not included in the family of God, they belong to the godless 'world' (in the sense of 2. 15–17; 3. 1), which lies in the grip of 'the evil one', called in the Gospel 'the ruler of this world' (John 14. 30). As this ruler, on Jesus' own testimony, has no authority over Him, so he has none over those who by faith share in Jesus' victory over the world. But those who are still dominated by the standards of the world organized without reference to God are enslaved by its ruler and cannot share in the victory which has overcome him. This passing world order and its ruler are on their way out, to be superseded by the eternal order and *its* Ruler; the subjects of the latter will abide for ever (cf. 2. 17).

In the world which God created man has been made in his Creator's image to represent Him to the rest of the created world. But man has abdicated his dominion over the world as God's representative in favour of a dominion which he imagines is autonomous, but which in fact has let in the powers of evil and anarchy. Nevertheless the created world, as distinct from the transient world order, remains God's world, and through the Son whom the Father sent as Saviour of the world (4. 14) man's rightful dominion under God is to be re-established and the usurpation of 'the evil one' brought to an end.[23]

The third thing that 'we know' is that 'the Son of God has come' – 'come in flesh', that is to say (4. 2), come moreover 'through water and blood' (5. 6) – and has given us spiritual intelligence, a faculty of perception or apprehension (Gr. *dianoia*) which far surpasses the 'knowledge' cultivated by the Gnostic seceders, for through it we come to the personal knowledge not only of truth in the abstract (2. 21) but of 'the True One' Himself. Whether, as 'fathers', they know Him as the One who is 'from the beginning' or, as 'children', know Him as 'the Father' (2. 13 f.), it is through the Son of God that they have acquired this knowledge: *He* has made known the God whom no one has ever seen (John 1. 18).

V. 20b **and we are in him that is true,** *even* **in his Son Jesus Christ. This is the true God, and eternal life.** v. 21 *My* **little children, guard yourselves from idols.**

Not only has the Son of God made the true God known; through faith-union with Him His people have their being in 'the True One'. To abide in the Father and to abide in the Son are two ways of stating the one experience: 'if what you heard from the beginning abides in you', John has already told them, 'then you will abide in the Son and in the Father' (2. 24). It may be that the seceders claimed a special part in the Father, but since they denied the Son His true status, their claim was disallowed, for it is only through the Son that men and women may dwell in God, just as it is only through the Son that God is pleased to dwell in men. 'If a man loves me', says Jesus in the Fourth Gospel, 'he will keep my word, and my Father will love him, and we will come to him and make our home (*monē*, cognate with *menō*, 'abide') with him' (John 14. 23). John, in closing, takes up the theme of his opening paragraph, where he assured his readers that the fellowship which he shared with them was fellowship 'with the Father and with his Son Jesus Christ'. As in the prologue to the letter Jesus Christ is described as 'the Eternal Life which was the Father and was made manifest to us', so here He is characterized as 'the true God and eternal life'. So fully is the Father expressed in His Son that what is predicated of the former can be predicated of the latter: 'what God was, the Word was' (John 1. 1, NEB). Our Lord is rightly acclaimed as 'true God of true God'; as C. K. Barrett says in commenting on the first verse of the Gospel of John: 'The deeds and words of Jesus are the deeds and words of God; if this be not true the book is blasphemous'.[24] Since, then, it is only in the true God and in His Son Jesus Christ that eternal life resides, it is urgently necessary to distinguish truth from error. The 'idols' or false appearances (Gr. *eidōla*) against which John warns his readers to be on their guard are not material images; they are false conceptions of God.[25] Any conception of Him that is at variance with His self-revelation in Christ is an idol. Hence, says John, since you have received the truth, have nothing to do with counterfeits; beware of imitations and refuse all substitutes.[26]

NOTE ON THE 'THREE HEAVENLY WITNESSES'

The sentence which appears in the AV as 1 John 5. 7 ('For there are three that bear record in heaven, the Father, the Word, and the Holy Ghost; and these three are one') is no part of the original text of the letter. It appears in a treatise written by Priscillian (a Spanish Christian executed on a charge of heresy in AD 385) or by one of his followers.[27] It may have originated as a comment on the authentic passage about the three witnesses (1 John 5. 8); at any rate in the course of the fifth century it was incorporated from the margin into the text of an Old Latin (pre-Vulgate) manuscript. It was not incorporated into the text of the Vulgate until about AD 800, but once incorporated it remained there securely, and the balancing words 'in earth' were added in the following sentence. When Erasmus published his first printed edition of the Greek New Testament (1516) he was attacked for omitting the 'three heavenly witnesses', but he replied reasonably enough that he found them in no Greek manuscript. Rather incautiously he added that, if a Greek manuscript could be produced which contained the passage, he would include it. In due course such a Greek manuscript was produced – by no means an ancient one, for it was written about 1520! Erasmus knew that this was no evidence at all – the passage had plainly been translated into Greek from the Latin Vulgate by the writer of this manuscript – but he had given his promise, and he was a man of peace, so in his next edition (the third edition, 1522) he included it, adding a footnote in which he complained that the manuscript had been written with the express purpose of putting him on the spot. From Erasmus's third edition the passage was translated into German (by Luther) and into English (by Tyndale); it was taken over into other early printed editions of the Greek New Testament, and hence appears in the 'Received Text' and in the Authorized Version.

The Greek manuscript which was produced for the discomfiture of Erasmus is now in the library of Trinity College, Dublin.[28] Today we know of three other Greek manuscripts which contain the passage: one of the fifteenth century,[29] one of the sixteenth,[30] and another in which it is added in a seventeenth-century hand in the margin of a twelfth-century manuscript.[31]

The official Sixto-Clementine edition of the Vulgate published in 1592 contained the passage, and therefore its authenticity was for long accepted *de rigueur* in the Roman Catholic Church. In 1897 the Holy Office issued a ruling, confirmed by Pope Leo XIII, that the genuineness of the passage could not be safely denied. The American 'Confraternity Edition' of the English New Testament (a revision of the Rheims-Challoner version), published in 1941, included it;[32] a footnote points out that 'according to the evidence of many manuscripts, and the majority of commentators', it does not belong to the true text, but adds: 'The Holy See reserves to itself the right to pass finally on the origin of the present reading' (i.e. the reading which preserves the reference to the three heavenly witnesses). As late as 1945, it was included in the translation of the New Testament prepared by R. A. Knox under archiepiscopal direction; a footnote was added: 'This verse does not occur in any good Greek manuscript. But the Latin manuscripts may have preserved the true text'. In fact, the best Latin manuscripts also lack the verse. It is perhaps a measure of the advance made in twenty years that the verse is absent both from the Catholic Edition of the RSV (1965) and from the Jerusalem Bible (1966). There are one or two Protestant quarters where rearguard actions in defence of the verse are still attempted, but evidence is evidence.

Although the verse came to be valued as a proof-text for the doctrine of the Trinity when once its place in the Vulgate and 'Received' texts was established, the validity of this doctrine is completely independent of it. The classic formulations of Nicaea (325), Constantinople (381) and Chalcedon (451) were the work of theologians who knew nothing of the 'three heavenly witnesses'.

NOTES

1. G. G. Findlay, *Fellowship in the Life Eternal* (London, 1909), p. 368.
2. Confessing Jesus to be the Son of God is tantamount to confessing Him to be the Christ (1 John 2. 22; 5. 1); the twofold formulation is brought together by the Evangelist in John 20. 31: 'that you may believe that Jesus is the Christ, the Son of God' – where the designation 'the Christ' may be

appropriate to Jewish readers (cf. W. C. van Unnik, 'The Purpose of St. John's Gospel', in *The Gospels Reconsidered*, Oxford, 1960, pp. 167 ff.) and the designation 'the Son of God' (i.e. the One in whom God is fully revealed) for Gentile readers.

3. Cf. Augustine, *Against Maximin* ii. 22. 3. J. Massingberd Ford (' "Mingled Blood" from the Side of Christ', *NTS* 15, 1968–69, pp. 337 f.) sees in John 19. 34 a reference to Jesus as the Passover Lamb, and 'cannot correlate this interpretation to any other references to water and blood in the Johannine corpus' (namely those in 1 John 5. 6, 8).

4. So Tertullian, *On Baptism*, 16. Several authorities, including Codices Sinaiticus and Alexandrinus, with a few minuscules and some editions of the Latin, Syriac and Coptic versions, read 'water and blood and Spirit', adding the witness of Pentecost to that of the baptism and the passion.

5. The preposition translated 'by' in the first half of the verse is *dia* ('through', 'by means of'); that translated 'with' three times in the second half of the verse is *en* (used in its instrumental sense, which is practically synonymous with *dia* followed by the genitive).

6. J. Calvin takes a different line: 'I do not doubt that by the words "water and blood" he refers to the ancient rites of the Law' (*Commentary on John 11–21 and 1 John*, trans. T. H. L. Parker, Edinburgh, 1961, p. 302).

7. His witness in Scripture is a material factor in the confirmation of the physical death of Jesus in John 19. 36 f.

8. The Latin Vulgate probably bears witness to a text which omitted the second occurrence of 'Spirit' and read: 'And it is the Spirit that bears witness that he (i.e. Christ) is the truth'.

9. The words 'in earth' following 'there are three that bear witness' in AV are a late addition made necessary by the insertion of the spurious text about the three that bear witness 'in heaven' immediately before verse 8. See pp. 129 f.

10. *Die Tradition und der Charakter des ersten Johannesbriefes* (Tübingen, 1957), pp. 147 ff.; cf. T. W. Manson, 'Entry into Membership of the Early Church', *JTS* 48 (1947), pp. 25 ff. Manson points to the case of Cornelius and his household, who received the Spirit (evidenced by their speaking with tongues) before baptism (Acts 10. 44–48; contrast the order in Acts 2. 38; 8. 15 f.; 19. 5 f.), and suggests that Paul regarded the utterance of 'Abba Father!' (Rom. 8. 15 f.; Gal. 4. 6) or 'Jesus is Lord!' (Rom. 10. 9; 1 Cor. 12. 3) as sufficient evidence of reception of the Spirit to satisfy the requirements for baptism.

11. This is a Jewish missionary document of Essene affinities, in which the name of Joseph's Egyptian wife Asenath is given a Hebrew spelling and etymology Aseneth, perhaps to make it mean 'female Essene' ('Esseness'). She is treated as a proselyte, and undergoes an initiation in which 'anointing' (or 'renewal by God's Holy Spirit') is accompanied by the 'eating of the bread of life' and 'the drinking of the blessed cup of immortality'. Apart from the 'anointing', this has little enough relevance to 1 John.

12. In the early Christian recension of the pseudepigraphic *Testament of Levi* (one of the *Testaments of the Twelve Patriarchs*) Levi describes how 'seven men in white raiment' install him in the priestly office: 'the first anointed me with holy oil, . . . the second washed me with pure water and fed me with bread and wine . . .' (8. 4 f.) – in which the influence of this threefold Christian initiation has been detected (cf. T. W. Manson, 'Miscellanea Apocalyptica III', *JTS* 48, 1947, pp. 59 ff.).

13. Gr. *pisteuō eis*, as in John 3. 36, etc.; see notes on 3. 23 (p. 100) and 5. 13 (pp. 122 f.).

14. The reading of AV, RSV, NEB, 'in himself' (Gr. *en hautō* or *en heautō*), is preferable in this context to RV 'in him' (Gr. *en autō*); the difference in Greek may hang on nothing more than the presence or absence of an aspirate, not marked in uncial writing.

15. Manuscript authorities are divided between the present *pisteuēte* ('that you may hold the faith', NEB text) and the aorist *pisteusēte* ('that you may come to believe', NEB margin).

16. Gr. *pisteuō eis*, as in John 1. 12; 2. 23; 3. 18, etc.; see notes on 3. 23 (p. 100) and 5. 10 (p. 121).

17. *Lectures to my Students*, abridged one-volume edition (London, 1954), p. 65.

18. RSV renders 'sin unto death' as 'mortal sin'; NEB as 'deadly sin' – possibly (but not certainly) in allusion to Article XVI: 'Not every deadly sin willingly committed after baptism, is sin against the Holy Ghost, and unpardonable...'.

19. The rendering 'not concerning this do I say that he should make request' is a flagrant example of RV pedantry; it is more appropriate to a schoolboy's 'crib' than to a version of the Bible intended for public use.

20. Yet another suggestion is that he means a sin which, like the 'high-handed' sin of Num. 15. 30, can be expiated only by death; this is improbable.

21. Heb. 6. 4–6; cf. Heb. 10. 26–29. Others have compared the sentence passed by our Lord against those who attributed His power to expel demons to possession by Beelzebul instead of to the Spirit of God (Matt. 12. 28): 'whoever blasphemes against the Holy Spirit never has forgiveness, but is guilty of an eternal sin' (Mark 3. 29). They too were guilty of a deliberate refusal of the witness of God.

22. Similarly TEV: 'We know that no child of God keeps on sinning, for the Son of God keeps him safe, and the Evil One cannot harm him'.

23. Cf. Rom. 8. 19 ff.

24. C. K. Barrett, *The Gospel according to St. John* (London, 1955), p. 130.

25. Are all 'conceptions' of God false, falling under the general ban on 'graven images'? The son of a colleague of mine, directed in his Divinity class at school to write an essay on 'My Concept of God', queried the appropriateness of the subject: 'My father says that any concept of God is an idol', he told his teacher. That is certainly true if we allow any concept or conception of God to take the place of God Himself.

26. The Byzantine witnesses and Received Text add 'Amen' (so AV). This is probably due to liturgical usage when the public reading of the epistle in church was concluded with 'Amen'.

27. Instantius, according to G. Morin, 'Pro Instantio', *Revue Bénédictine* 30 (1913), pp. 153 ff.; but cf. the reply by J. Martin, 'Priscillianus oder Instantius?' in *Historisches Jahrbuch der Dörres-Gesellschaft* 47 (1927), pp. 237 ff. The treatise is the *Liber Apologeticus* (Tract. 1. 4; *CSEL* xvii. 6): 'as John says, "there are three that say witness in earth, the Spirit, the water and the blood, and these three (agree) in one; and there are three that say witness in heaven, the Father, the Word and the Spirit, and these three are one in Christ Jesus"' (from which it will be seen that the intrusive words originally *followed* the authentic text about the three witnesses).

28. In the catalogue of Greek NT minuscules its serial number is now 61.

29. Minuscule 629.

30. A manuscript copy of the Greek text of the Complutensian Polyglot, which included the passage (translated, of course, from Latin) when it was printed in 1513–14.

31. Minuscule 88. See B. M. Metzger, *The Text of the New Testament* (Oxford, 1964), pp. 101 f.

32. This was because of the Vulgate basis of the Confraternity Version of 1941. The revised edition of 1970 – in The New American Bible – is based on the scientifically established Greek text.

THE SECOND EPISTLE OF JOHN

INTRODUCTION AND ANALYSIS

The second and third Epistles of John present us with the closest approximations in the New Testament to the conventional letter-form of the contemporary Graeco-Roman world.[1] The second epistle, which deals with the same general problem as the first epistle, but apparently in reference to the particular situation of one local group or house-church, lends itself readily to the following analysis:

1 Opening salutation (verses 1–3)
2 Occasion of rejoicing (verse 4)
3 Exhortation (verses 5–11)
4 Personal notes (verse 12)
5 Final greeting (verse 13)

TEXT AND EXPOSITION

I OPENING SALUTATION (verses 1–3)

**V. 1 The elder unto the elect lady and her children, whom
I love in truth; and not I only, but also all they that know the
truth;**

We are confronted immediately by the twin problems of the
identity of the writer and that of the recipients. 'The elder' is the
writer's self-chosen designation both here and in 3 John. We are
hardly to think here of an elder in the sense which the word
presbyteros usually bears in Christian contexts in the New Testament, that is, one who discharges the ministry of eldership in a
local church. In this sense there were several elders in each church,
and it would be strange to find one of them singling himself out
with the designation 'the elder' and addressing other churches
with authority. The word appears in another specialized sense in
second-century Christian literature, of church leaders in the
generation after the apostles, particularly those who were disciples
of apostles or of 'apostolic men', and were therefore guarantors of
the 'tradition' which they received from the apostles and delivered
in turn to their own followers.[2] This sense may have been
borrowed from the Old Testament references to 'the elders who
outlived Joshua' (Josh. 24. 31; Judg. 2. 7). Irenaeus, for example,
mentions what he heard 'from a certain elder (presbyter), who had
heard it from those who had seen the apostles, and from those
who learned it (from them)',[3] and cites him again as 'the elder';[4]
later he quotes 'an elder, a disciple of the apostles',[5] who appears
to have been in even closer touch with the fountain-head of
Christian teaching, and is probably to be identified with one at
whose feet Irenaeus sat in his boyhood, Polycarp of Smyrna, who
in his turn had been acquainted with 'John and the others who had
seen the Lord'.[6] Irenaeus's other 'elder', whose contact with the
apostles was indirect, may have been his predecessor as bishop of

Lyons, Pothinus, who died a martyr in AD 177 when he was over ninety years old.

Papias, bishop of Hierapolis in Phrygia, half a century older than Irenaeus, who calls him 'an ancient (*archaios*) man',[7] and a contemporary of Polycarp, also has something to say of the elders, from whom he eagerly collected whatever they could tell him of the teaching of Jesus. 'If ever a person came my way who had been a companion of the elders', he adds, 'I would enquire about the sayings of the elders: "What did Andrew or Peter, or Philip, or Thomas or James, or John or Matthew or any other of the Lord's disciples say? And what do Aristion and the elder John, the disciples of the Lord, say?" For I did not suppose that what I could get from books was of such great value to me as the utterances of a living and abiding voice'.[8]

The relation between Papias's two references to John has provided material for much inconclusive debate. Does he refer to two men called John, both 'disciples of the Lord' (as such orthodox scholars as J. B. Lightfoot[9] and S. P. Tregelles[10] thought, together with many others since their time), or to one only?[11] Whichever is the true answer to this question, it may have little relevance for the exegesis of this epistle and the following one. Papias also quotes one of his elders as 'the elder' *par excellence*; for example, the information he gives about the origin of the Gospel of Mark is said to be what 'the elder' used to say.[12] This suggests that in Papias's circle there was one senior man who because of his age, experience and authority was referred to in this way. It is quite likely that the self-designation of the writer of 2 and 3 John is to be similarly explained – not that he was *necessarily* identical with Papias's 'elder', but that in the circle in which he was best known he was given the affectionate and respectful title 'the elder' both because he was older than the other members of the circle and because his personal knowledge of the Way went back so much farther than theirs. If to them he was 'the elder', to him they may well have been his 'little children', as the anonymous author of 1 John calls his readers. That all three epistles come from one and the same writer is, in my judgment, scarcely to be doubted.

The identity of the recipients, 'the elect lady and her children', presents a problem of another kind. The *prima facie* picture is of a Christian *materfamilias* some at least of whose children follow the truth in which they were brought up and to whom greetings are sent from her nephews and nieces in the place from which 'the elder' is writing. Attempts have been made to extract her personal name from the designation which the writer gives her – *eklektē kyria*. Might this be rendered 'the elect Kyria' or (less probably) 'the lady Electa'?[13] She is evidently well known to Christians in many places: she is loved by all who 'know the truth'. No individual traits appear throughout the letter, however; in this respect it forms a contrast with 3 John, in which we have vivid thumb-nail sketches of Gaius, the recipient, and of Diotrephes and Demetrius, about whom the writer has something to say. Such considerations have led many interpreters, from the fourth century onwards, to understand 'the elect lady' as a corporate personality. As a city or country was commonly personified as a woman, like 'the daughter of Zion' in the Old Testament prophets or Britannia on British coins[14] (a representation going back to Roman times), so a church might be personified – whether the Church Catholic (portrayed in Rev. 20. 2, 9, 'as a bride adorned for her husband') or a local church (as probably in 1 Pet. 5. 13, where 'she who is at Babylon' is best understood as an elect sister-church of those to whom the letter is addressed). If this interpretation be followed here, then 'the elect lady' is a local church (not the Church Catholic, for the Church Catholic has no sister), 'her children' (*tekna*) are the members of that church, and the 'children' (*tekna*) of her 'elect sister' (v. 13) are the members of the local church in the place where the writer is resident. The weighing up of the probabilities for the individual or corporate character of the 'lady' is part of the exegesis of the letter. If the following exegesis leans to the corporate interpretation, this does not suggest that finality is attainable on this question; so long as either interpretation claims the support of serious students of the document, the question must be treated as an open one.

The 'lady and her children' are assured that the writer loves them 'in truth' (cf. 3 John 1); this probably means not only that he loves them truly (cf. 1 John 3. 18) but that he loves them as a fellow-believer, as one who, together with them, is 'of the truth' (cf. 1 John 3. 19). And all who are similarly 'of the truth', all who 'know the truth' – the truth as embodied in Him who is the truth (John 14. 6)[15] – share with the writer in loving them too.

V. 2 for the truth's sake which abideth in us, and it shall be with us for ever:

This language is reminiscent of the words in which our Lord promises His Spirit to the disciples in the upper room: 'he abides with you and is (or will be)[16] in you' (John 14. 17). There is nothing surprising if what is said of the Spirit in one place is said of 'the truth' in another place: 'it is the Spirit that bears witness, because the Spirit is the truth' (1 John 5. 7). It is through 'the Spirit of truth' that He who is Truth incarnate dwells perpetually in and with His people.

V. 3 Grace, mercy, peace shall be with us, from God the Father, and from Jesus Christ, the Son of the Father, in truth and love.

The threefold 'Grace, mercy, peace' in the opening salutation appears also in 1 and 2 Timothy. Jude has a comparable salutation, 'mercy, peace and love'; the earlier Pauline letters and Titus have the twofold 'Grace and peace', as also have the two Petrine letters and John's salutation to the churches of Asia (Rev. 1. 4). The future indicative 'shall be' is perhaps due to the influence of the same form in verse 2. According to Westcott, 'the succession "grace, mercy, peace" marks the order from the first motion of God to the final satisfaction of man'.[17] The phrase 'Jesus Christ, the Son of the Father', is unique, but the truth it expresses is attested throughout the New Testament and is basic to John's argument (cf. verse 9; 1 John 2. 23). The addition 'Lord' (kyrios) before 'Jesus Christ' in the Received Text and AV is not original;

it is noteworthy that this title is not given to Jesus (nor used in any other sense[18]) anywhere in these three epistles. Where 'truth and love' coexist harmoniously, we have a well-balanced Christian character (cf. Eph. 4. 15).

2   OCCASION OF REJOICING (verse 4)

V. 4   **I rejoice greatly that I have found** *certain* **of thy children walking in truth, even as we received commandment from the Father.**

'I rejoice' is aorist in Greek (*echarēn*); attention is thus concentrated on the moment when the elder's joy began, but since his joy persists we may follow RV and render by the English present.[19] The phrase '(certain) of thy children' (*tekna*) reflects the Greek use of the preposition *ek* in a partitive sense (*ek tōn teknōn sou*); an indefinite pronoun like 'certain' or 'some' is required to complete the sense in idiomatic modern English, although Greek can dispense with it. Since there is no definite article before 'truth' it may be held that 'walking in truth' here means simply 'conducting themselves in all sincerity', whereas the article would point to the embodiment of truth in Christ. It is doubtful if such a sharp distinction can be maintained; if they conducted themselves in sincerity, they conducted themselves as befits followers of Christ, and since their conduct was in accordance with the 'commandment' given them by the Father, it was as much 'walking in love' as 'walking in truth'. The Father's 'commandment' is communicated through the Son (cf. 1 John 3. 23). John does not necessarily suggest that the elect lady's other children do not so conduct themselves; in using the partitive construction he refers to some of them whom he had actually met, away from the place where the 'lady' was normally resident. His joy at meeting them was such that he determined to write a letter to their 'mother', that is (on the premise adopted in this exposition) to the local church from which they had come.

3 EXHORTATION (verses 5–11)

V. 5 And now I beseech thee, lady, not as though I wrote to thee a new commandment, but that which we had from the beginning, that we love one another. v. 6 And this is love, that we should walk after his commandments. This is the commandment, even as ye heard from the beginning, that ye should walk in it.

The exhortation follows closely that given in general terms in the first epistle. Since John was so delighted to find some members of the community keeping the great commandment, his desire was that the whole community should continue to keep it. For the description of the commandment of love as no 'new commandment,' but one 'which we had from the beginning', cf. 1 John 2. 7.[20] For the essence of love as the keeping of God's commandments cf. 1 John 5. 3. To 'walk in it' at the end of verse 6 probably means to walk in love; so RSV: 'that you follow love' (NEB takes 'it' to refer to 'the commandment': 'This is the command which was given you from the beginning, to be your rule of life'). We have the same emphasis on love as in the first epistle, the same identification of love and obedience, the same insistence on what has been held 'from the beginning'.

V. 7 For many deceivers are gone forth into the world, *even* they that confess not that Jesus Christ cometh in the flesh. This is the deceiver and the antichrist.

This repeats the warning against 'many Antichrists' given in 1 John 2. 18 ff.; 4. 1–6. The 'deceivers' (*planoi*) are those who lead people astray (cf. the verb *planaō* in 1 John 2. 26). They are described, literally, as those 'who do not acknowledge Jesus Christ coming in flesh'; the participle is present here (*erchomenon*), whereas in 1 John 4. 2 it is perfect (*elēlythota*), but the reference is, as there, to the Docetic denial of our Lord's incarnation; the Greek construction here may be more freely, but idiomatically,

rendered with RSV: 'men who will not acknowledge[21] the coming
of Jesus Christ in the flesh'. The RV rendering, 'they that confess
not that Jesus Christ cometh in the flesh', might be misunderstood
as a reference to the Second Advent.[22]

V. 8 Look to yourselves, that ye [1]lose not the things which [2]we have wrought, but that ye receive a full reward.

> [1] Or, *destroy.*
> [2] Many ancient authorities read *ye.*

To pay attention to such deceivers and follow them on the path
of error would involve the waste of all their Christian service
hitherto and the loss of the fruit properly accruing from it. In
place of AV and RV 'we have wrought',[23] which is followed by NEB
('that you may not lose all that we worked for'), there is a variant
reading 'you have wrought'[24] (cf. RSV 'you have worked for'),
which is more appropriate in the context. If, rejecting the entice-
ment of error, they maintained the teaching which they had heard
'from the beginning' and continued the work they had been doing
thus far, they would be paid their reward in full. This exhortation
echoes much that is taught in other New Testament writings;
compare I Cor. 3. 8, 14; Rev. 22. 12.

V. 9 Whosoever [1]goeth onward and abideth not in the teaching of Christ, hath not God: he that abideth in the teaching, the same hath both the Father and the Son. v. 10 If any one cometh unto you, and bringeth not this teaching, receive him not into *your* house, and give him no greeting: v. 11 for he that giveth him greeting partaketh in his evil works.

> [1] Or, *taketh the lead.*

The Docetist teacher 'goes on' beyond the apostolic teaching;
his 'advanced teaching' is condemned because it is 'advanced' in
this sense. The apostolic teaching could be called 'the teaching of
Christ' either because it is the teaching which derives from Christ
and is vested with His authority[25] or because it is the authoritative
and true teaching about Christ. Either interpretation would be

appropriate; whether we accept the former or the latter depends
on our understanding the genitive 'of Christ' as subjective or
objective genitive respectively. There is a strong balance of
probability in favour of the former construction (so Westcott).
Anyone, then, who has advanced beyond this teaching in a Docetic
direction 'has not God', since 'no one who denies the Son has the
Father' (1 John 2. 23a); everyone who 'abides' in it 'has both
the Father and the Son', since 'he who confesses the Son has the
Father also' (1 John 2. 23b). The injunction not to receive any one
who does not bring 'the teaching of Christ' means that no such
person must be accepted as a Christian teacher or as one entitled
to the fellowship of the church. It does not mean that (say) one of
Jehovah's Witnesses should not be invited into the house for a
cup of tea in order to be shown the way of God more perfectly in
the sitting-room than would be convenient on the doorstep. Still
less does it mean that disagreements on church order should be
treated as deviations from 'the teaching of Christ' and used as a
ground of exclusion from social as well as ecclesiastical fellowship,
as was done by Edward Cronin in 1849 in a letter terminating 'an
unbroken intimacy and friendship of twenty-five years' with
Anthony Norris Groves.[26] But for a church, or its responsible
leaders, knowingly to admit within its bounds the propagation of
teaching subversive of the gospel is to participate in what John
describes as 'evil works'. To give one who brings such teaching a
greeting is to say *chaire* to him, to bid him hail when he arrives or
farewell when he leaves – here the former is more probably in
view. It is plain from the early Christian manual called the
Didache or *Teaching of the Twelve Apostles* (a work compiled not
much, if at all, later than the Epistles of John) that travelling
prophets and apostles were well-known figures in church life at
this period, and it was necessary to distinguish the right kind from
the wrong kind. The *Didache* gives priority to the doctrinal
criterion. After summarizing the 'way of life' and the 'way of
death' and the proper procedure for baptism, fasting and the
Eucharist, it goes on: 'Whosoever then comes and teaches you
all these things aforesaid, receive him. If, however, the teacher

himself is perverted and teaches another doctrine to destroy these
things, do not listen to him; but if his teaching promotes righteousness and the knowledge of the Lord, receive him as the Lord'.[27]
It also lays down some practical and pedestrian rules of thumb ('if
he stays three days, he is a false prophet . . . if he asks for money,
he is a false prophet').[28] The crucial test has already been laid
down in 1 John 4. 1–3, and this is the test which is recommended
to 'the elect lady'.

4 PERSONAL NOTES (verse 12)

V. 12   Having many things to write unto you, I would not
write them **with paper and ink: but I hope to come unto you,**
and to speak face to face, that your joy may be fulfilled.

Unfortunately we do not know for sure what the other things
were which the Elder wanted to say to these friends; perhaps he
wished to deal in greater detail, in reference to specific persons,
with those questions which are treated briefly and in principle in
the letter. The 'paper' which he mentions is papyrus (Gr. *chartēs*);
a short letter like 2 John would be accommodated on one papyrus
sheet of normal size. To 'speak face to face' is literally 'to speak
mouth to mouth' (Gr. *stoma pros stoma*) – a biblical phrase; God
uses it of His converse with Moses in Num. 12. 8.[29] The clause
'that your joy may be fulfilled' is repeated from 1 John 1. 4; in
both places there is textual variation between 'your' and 'our'
('our' is read here by AV, RSV and NEB and is probably to be
preferred, as in 1 John 1. 4).[30]

5 FINAL GREETING (verse 13)

V. 13   The children of thine elect sister salute thee.

The status of the lady's 'elect sister' will be comparable to her
own status; if she is a local church, so is her sister (the church in
the place where the Elder happens to be at the time of writing).
The greetings are sent to the lady by 'the children' of her 'elect
sister'; if the sisters are two churches and the 'children' their

respective members, then the singular and plural are practically interchangeable. It is useless to speculate why the greetings are sent by the sister's 'children' rather than by herself; the Elder can scarcely be referring to sympathetic members of a church whose official leadership is unsympathetic, for in that case he would hardly describe the church as 'elect'. One minuscule of the eleventh century (Cod. 465) identifies the 'elect sister' as the church of Ephesus; this is a piece of traditional interpretation with no textual authority.[31] But both 'sisters' were probably churches in that neighbourhood.[32]

NOTES

1. Cf. R. W. Funk, 'The Form and Structure of II and III John', *JBL* 86 (1967), pp. 424 ff.
2. Cf. Irenaeus, *Against Heresies* v. 5. 1; 36. 1 f.; *Demonstration* 3; 61; also Hippolytus, passages cited by A. Hamel, *Kirche bei Hippolyt von Rom* (Gütersloh, 1951), pp. 106 f. In *Against Heresies* iv. 27–32 Irenaeus incorporates an anti-Marcionite defence by an 'elder' of the unity of the Creator with the Father revealed by Jesus; the OT and NT quotations woven into it indicate the important part played by such 'elders' in the development of the Canon between Papias and Irenaeus (see G. Bornkamm, in *TDNT* vi, Grand Rapids, 1969, pp. 670 ff., *s.v.* πρέσβυς, πρεσβύτερος).
3. *Against Heresies* iv. 42. 2.
4. *Against Heresies* iv. 46. 1; 47. 1.
5. *Against Heresies* iv. 49. 1.
6. *Letter to Florinus*, quoted by Eusebius, *Hist. Eccl.* v. 20. 6; see p. 22, n. 4. Cf. Irenaeus, *Against Heresies* ii. 22. 5; v. 30. 1; 33. 3 f., for the relation of the 'elders' to 'John, the disciple of the Lord'.
7. *Against Heresies* v. 33. 4 (see p. 22, n. 5). The adjective *archaios* suggests contact with the beginning (*archē*); cf. its application to Mnason in Acts 21. 16.
8. *Exegesis of the Dominical Oracles*, quoted by Eusebius, *Hist. Eccl.* iii. 39. 3 f. See p. 22, n. 5.
9. *Essays on the Work entitled 'Supernatural Religion'* (London, 1889), p. 144.
10. *The Historic Evidence of the Authorship and Transmission of the Books of the New Testament*[2] (London, 1881), p. 47.
11. E.g. F. W. Farrar, *The Early Days of Christianity* (London, 1882), pp. 618 ff.; G. Salmon, *Historical Introduction to the . . . New Testament*[4] (London, 1889), pp. 287 ff.; T. Zahn, *Apostel und Apostelschüler in der Provinz Asien* (Leipzig, 1900), pp. 112 ff., and *Introduction to the New Testament* (Edinburgh, 1909), ii, pp. 451 ff.; J. Chapman, *John the Presbyter and the Fourth Gospel* (Oxford, 1911); C. J. Cadoux, *Ancient Smyrna* (Oxford, 1938), pp. 316 f.
12. 'This also the elder used to say: "Mark became Peter's interpreter, and wrote down accurately all that he remembered, whether sayings or doings of Christ – not, however, in order, for he was neither a hearer nor a companion of the Lord, but afterwards, as I said, he accompanied Peter, who adapted his teachings as necessity required, not as though he were

making a compilation of the oracles of the Lord. So then, Mark made no mistake in writing certain things just as he remembered them, for he paid attention to one thing – not to omit anything he had heard, nor to include any false statement among them" ' (quoted by Eusebius, *Hist. Eccl.* iii. 39. 15). (It is possible that the two occurrences of 'he [Mark] remembered' should be rendered 'he [Peter] mentioned'.) It is uncertain if the same elder was Papias's authority for his further statement that 'Matthew compiled the oracles (*logia*) in the Hebrew speech, and everyone translated them as best he could' (*Hist. Eccl.* iii. 39. 16).

13. Clement of Alexandria took Electa (Eklektē) to be the lady's personal name, and (linking this passage with 1 Pet. 5. 13) concluded that she and her children were Babylonians and therefore, in view of the political situation at the time, Parthians (*Adumbrations* iv. 437). Hence the spurious title 'To the Parthians' was affixed to 2 John and then to the three Johannine letters as a group and so to 1 John (see p. 32, n. 1).

14. Cf. also the disconsolate female figure 'Captive Judaea' on Roman coins celebrating the fall of Jerusalem and suppression of the Jewish revolt.

15. Cf. also 1 John 5. 20, 'we know him that is true'.

16. Witnesses to the text read variously *esti* ('is') and *estai* ('will be').

17. *The Epistles of St. John* (London, 1902), p. 225.

18. The nearest approach to *kyrios* in these epistles is the courtesy use of the feminine *kyria* in 2 John 1, 5.

19. AV, RSV 'I rejoiced'; cf. NEB 'I was delighted'. Compare 3 John 3 (p. 148).

20. But see also 1 John 2. 8 (pp. 53 ff.).

21. The rendering 'who will not acknowledge . . .' (rather than 'who do not acknowledge . . .') is probably intended to bring out the force of the negative *mē* (not *ouch*) before the participle *homologountes*.

22. His *parousia* is not 'in flesh' but 'in glory'.

23. So Codex Vaticanus (first hand) with the bulk of Byzantine manuscripts and the Received Text.

24. So Codices Sinaiticus, Alexandrinus, 1739, and the Latin and Syriac versions.

25. See pp. 17 f. with p. 24, n. 14.

26. G. H. Lang, *Anthony Norris Groves* (London, 1939), p. 265.

27. *Didache* 11. 1 f. (cf. p. 149).

28. *Didache* 11. 5 f.

29. But in Deut. 34. 10 the LORD is said to have known him 'face to face' (LXX *prosōpon kata prosōpon*). Another, and more sinister, occurrence of our present idiom is in Jer. 32. 4 (LXX 39. 4), where the captive Zedekiah and his captor Nebuchadrezzar speak 'mouth to mouth'.

30. 'Our' (Gr. *hēmōn*) is the reading of Codex Sinaiticus and the Received Text; 'your' (Gr. *hymōn*) of Codices Vaticanus and Alexandrinus and the majority of manuscripts. See p. 40 with p. 46, n. 10.

31. Compare R. Eisler's identification of the 'elect lady' with the church of Palestine (*The Enigma of the Fourth Gospel*, London, 1938, pp. 170 f.), which lacks even the benefit of tradition. J. V. Bartlet had earlier identified her with the church of Thyatira (*JTS* 6, 1905, pp. 204 ff.) and G. G. Findlay with the church of Pergamum (*Fellowship in the Life Eternal*, London, 1909, pp. 32 ff.).

32. At the end of the epistle a few late manuscripts add 'Grace be with you'; the Byzantine witnesses and Received Text (whence AV) add the liturgical 'Amen'.

THE THIRD EPISTLE OF JOHN

INTRODUCTION AND ANALYSIS

The third Epistle, being addressed by an individual to an individual, approximates even more closely than the second epistle to the regular pattern of letter-writing in the Graeco-Roman world of that day. It may be analysed thus:

1 Opening salutation and good wishes (verses 1–2)
2 Occasion of rejoicing (verses 3–4)
3 Appreciation of help given to travelling teachers (verses 5–8)
4 Diotrephes's unbrotherly conduct (verses 9–10)
5 Exhortation (verse 11)
6 Recommendation of Demetrius (verse 12)
7 Personal notes (verses 13–14)
8 Final greeting (verse 15).

The teaching which the writer wished to see accepted and maintained in the churches for which he felt special responsibility was conveyed not only by himself in person, whether orally or in letters, but also by travelling teachers who visited the churches with his recommendation. Gaius, to whom this letter is written, had shown these messengers hospitality; the church to which Gaius evidently belonged, however, had refused to receive them, at the instigation of one Diotrephes. Gaius is praised for his hospitality, but Diotrephes's unco-operative behaviour is deplored. Another of the writer's messengers, Demetrius, probably the bearer of this letter, is commended to Gaius's friendly interest.

TEXT AND EXPOSITION

1 Opening Salutation and Good Wishes (verses 1–2)

V. 1 The elder unto Gaius the beloved, whom I love in truth.

The significance of the self-designation 'the elder' has been discussed in the note on 2 John 1. Gaius was a common name in the Roman world; it was one of the eighteen names from which Roman parents could choose a *praenomen* for one of their sons. Elsewhere in the New Testament we meet Gaius of Corinth, Paul's host (Rom. 16. 23; 1 Cor. 1. 14), and Gaius of Derbe or (according to the Western text) Doberus, Paul's travelling companion (Acts 19. 29; 20. 4). There is no ground for associating the Gaius of 3 John with any other bearer of the name. The adjective clause, 'whom I love in truth', is practically identical with the wording of 2 John 1 (see the note on that verse).

V. 2 Beloved, I pray that in all things thou mayest prosper and be in health, even as thy soul prospereth.

The convention of wishing one's reader good health at the outset of a letter ('Hoping this finds you well, as it leaves me at present') is one of great antiquity. So regular was this sort of thing in Latin letters that it was customarily expressed by the use of initials, S V B E E V (*si uales, bene est; ego ualeo,* 'if you are well, that is good; I am well'). The elder adapts such conventional good wishes in a manner all his own: he knows from Gaius's way of life that his soul is in a healthy condition, and he prays that his bodily health and general prosperity may match the prosperity of his soul. The late Professor A. Rendle Short remarked that at one time it occurred to him that 3 John 2 would be a suitable text to inscribe over his name in his friends' autograph albums, until he

reflected that, so far as some of them were concerned, a prayer
that their general health might match their spiritual prosperity
could be interpreted as a prayer that they might require his
professional attendance. But if the elder's prayer for Gaius were
answered, health and prosperity would be his in abundance.

2   OCCASION OF REJOICING (verses 3–4)

V. 3   **For I ¹rejoiced greatly, when brethren came and bare
witness unto thy truth, even as thou walkest in truth.**

¹ Or, *rejoice greatly, when brethren come and bear witness.*

John's conviction about Gaius's spiritual health is based on the
news about Gaius brought to him by 'brethren' – probably those
whom (according to verses 5–8) Gaius had entertained hospitably.
These men, on their return, told John about Gaius's 'truth' – that
is, the loyalty to Christ and the gospel by which his life was
marked. Like those children of 'the elect lady' mentioned in 2
John 4, Gaius 'walked' – conducted himself – 'in truth'. John
knows that the report about Gaius corresponds to the reality, and
is filled with gladness on this account.¹ (The conjunction 'For' at
the beginning of the sentence is not found in all authorities for
the text,² but its presence is apt, as it draws attention to the reason
for John's assurance that Gaius's soul is in a prosperous condition.)

V. 4   **Greater ¹joy have I none than ²this, to hear of my
children walking in truth.**

¹ Some ancient authorities read *grace.*
² Or, *these* things, *that I may hear.*

For 'joy' (Gr. *charan*) Codex Vaticanus and a few other
witnesses have the less appropriate reading 'grace' (*charin*). (The
same variation occurs in 2 Cor. 1. 15.) The infinitive 'to hear' (so
RV, RSV, NEB) represents Gr. *hina akouō*. Although in classical
Greek *hina* with the subjunctive mood expresses purpose, this is
no longer invariably so in Hellenistic Greek, which provides
sufficient examples like the present (cf. John 17. 3) of the increasing
tendency to use this construction as an equivalent of the infinitive –

a tendency which led to the complete supersession of the original infinitive forms by this construction, as in modern Greek (where *hina* appears in the shortened form *na*). The elder reckons Gaius among his 'children' (*tekna*); this might suggest that Gaius was a convert of his, but in view of his designation of all to whom 1 John was sent as 'my little children', he may mean no more than that Gaius is one of many younger fellow-believers for whom he feels a fatherly concern and affection.

3 APPRECIATION OF HELP GIVEN TO TRAVELLING TEACHERS (verses 5–8)

V. 5 Beloved, thou doest a faithful work in whatsoever thou doest toward them that are brethren and strangers withal;

The ministry of travelling teachers (sometimes called 'apostles' or 'prophets'), as has been mentioned in the notes on 2 John, was a well-known feature of church life in Western Asia at the end of the first and beginning of the second century. It was a Christian duty – 'a faithful (or loyal) work' – to show such visitors hospitality, and this duty was none the less to be discharged faithfully because the opportunity to profit by it was seized by some charlatans. The *Didache*, in its pedestrian way, underlines the importance of receiving as the Lord Himself 'everyone who comes in the name of the Lord'; every true prophet or teacher is 'worthy of his food'[3] (cf. Matt. 10. 10). One group of such teachers evidently went out with the commendation of the elder and his associates, and it was some of them who spoke so well of Gaius. They were 'strangers', and he took them in, treating them as his *guests* (the same word *xenos* does duty in both senses).

V. 6 who bare witness to thy love before the church: whom thou wilt do well to set forward on their journey worthily of God:

In Gaius's case 'walking in truth' was synonymous with 'walking in love'. He showed his visitors Christian love, and when

they spoke of his reception of them in their report of their journey
to the church from which presumably they had set out (perhaps
the same church as is called 'your elect sister' in 2 John 13),
Gaius's hospitality became a matter of widespread renown. He
did not show hospitality in order to gain this renown – indeed, the
renown probably meant that demands on his hospitality greatly
increased – but thanks to their appreciative report of his kindness
his example has been an encouragement to many others. His
kindness was worthy of the God whom he and they alike served;
it was a reflection of God's own kindness (cf. 2 Sam. 9. 3, 'the
kindness of God'). The words 'thou wilt do well' are an idiomatic
form of conveying a request (cf. NEB: 'Please help them on their
journey') or expressing thanks in advance (cf. a similar expression
in the past tense in Acts 10. 33, where 'you have done well to
come' means 'thank you for coming').

V. 7   **because that for the sake of the Name they went
forth, taking nothing of the Gentiles.**

If the Old Testament contains one or two books which do not
mention the name of God, the New Testament contains one which
does not mention Christ by name – our present epistle. But if
Christ is not mentioned by name here, He is referred to in other
ways: for example, 'the Name' on behalf of which these brethren
'went forth' was the name of Christ, and it was in Christ's name
that Gaius had received them (cf. Mark 9. 37). As in Jewish
parlance 'The Name' is a surrogate for YHWH, so here 'The Name'
is a synonym for Christ. It was for His sake that these men went
forth on their teaching journeys, as it is for His sake that all true
Christian service is done. And when it is known to others that it
is done for His sake, His name is honoured. It was good on one
occasion to hear a Hindu resident in East Africa tell what a blessing
the sisters in a neighbouring mission hospital were to the area in
which they worked, and better still to hear him add: 'and they do
it all for Jesus Christ'. Since these teachers went out on their
journeys for Christ's sake, it was fitting that they should be

supported by Christ's people. Had they accepted hospitality from 'the Gentiles', it might have given the impression that their own people did not support them adequately. The word rendered 'Gentiles' here is *ethnikoi*, Gentile individuals (as in Matt. 5. 47; 6. 7; 18. 17), not the commoner *ethnē*, Gentile nations. It has been pointed out that there is in 3 John 'precisely the same *contrast* between the *ekklēsia* and the *ethnikoi* as in Matt. 18. 17: "If he refuses to listen even to the church, let him be to you an *ethnikos*".'[4]

V. 8 We therefore ought to welcome such, that we may be fellow-workers with the truth.

The pronoun 'we' is emphatic: since these men refused to seek help or hospitality from Gentiles, 'we Christians (*hēmeis*) ought to receive them into our homes and entertain them' (Gr. *hypolambanō*). If, as 2 John 10 f. says, to harbour a false teacher is to have fellowship with his 'wicked works', correspondingly to show hospitality to those who maintain the truth of the gospel is to co-operate 'with the truth', and to enjoy the fulfilment of our Lord's promise that 'he who receives a prophet in the name of a prophet will receive a prophet's reward' (Matt. 10. 41).

4 DIOTREPHES'S UNBROTHERLY CONDUCT (verses 9-10)

V. 9 I wrote somewhat unto the church: but Diotrephes, who loveth to have the preeminence among them, receiveth us not.

The most reliable authorities for the text have 'I wrote somewhat' (Gr. *ti*, 'something'); other readings are 'I would have written to the church',[5] 'I would have written something to the church',[6] 'I wrote to the church herself'[7] and 'I wrote unto the church' (so AV, following the Received Text). Of these variants, 'I would have written to the church' is the second best attested reading; if it were accepted, the implication would be that John is writing to Gaius instead of the church, because he knows that, thanks to the influence of Diotrephes, a letter to the church would be fruitless. But if we read (as certainly we should) 'I wrote somewhat', the question arises what he wrote and to which church. The suggestion has been made that here is a reference to 2 John – that, the elect lady herself being unresponsive, John had now to write to one of her children, Gaius.[8] But this is unlikely. The natural inference to draw from John's words here is that he had written earlier to Gaius's home church commending his travelling teachers; but this is not the subject of 2 John. On the other hand, the false teaching about which the writer is concerned in 2 John does not figure here. It is better to conclude that the letter to the church, to which reference is made in the present passage, is lost, although its tenor may be surmised.

However that may be, the letter failed of its intended effect because Diotrephes, a dominant personality in that church, forbade his brethren to comply with the Elder's request. Diotrephes is described as *ho philoprōteuōn autōn*, which RSV renders (quite literally) 'who likes to put himself first' and NEB (more freely) 'their would-be leader'. The language suggests a self-promoted demagogue rather than a constitutional *presbyteros* or *episkopos*. It is conceivable, of course, that even a constitutional leader might have been regarded by the Elder as no better than a trumped-up dictator if he behaved in the way described here. The question has been repeatedly raised of the relation which this reference bears to the monarchical episcopate, which we find beginning to emerge in the churches of Western Asia early in the second century, exemplified in such saints and martyrs as Ignatius of Antioch and Polycarp of Smyrna. C. H. Dodd sums up the alternatives thus: 'It may be (i) that Diotrephes is in fact the first "monarchical bishop" known to history in the province of Asia;[9] . . . it may be (ii) that Diotrephes is a symptom of the disease which the quasi-apostolic ministry of monarchical bishops was designed to relieve.'[10] On the whole, the second is more probable. The first monarchical bishops of whom we know were concerned, just as the Elder himself was, to maintain the apostolic teaching in their churches and to exclude whatever conflicted with it. Diotrephes is not charged with heresy,[11] and his exclusive behaviour may have been due entirely to his determination to allow no teaching or leadership in the church but his own. Twenty centuries of church history have witnessed many of his successors: the lust for power, from whatever form of inner insecurity it may spring, is always a curse, and pre-eminently so in the realm of religion. It is, however, possible that his conduct arose in some degree from his disapproval of the teaching that John and his friends maintained; we cannot be sure. He does not receive us, says John; that is to say, he neither recognized John's authority nor admitted his messengers to the church. The former sense comes to the fore in RSV: 'does not acknowledge my authority' (NEB, more generally, says 'will have nothing to do with us').

V. 10   Therefore, if I come, I will bring to remembrance his works which he doeth, prating against us with wicked words: and not content therewith, neither doth he himself receive the brethren, and them that would he forbiddeth, and casteth *them* out of the church.

Diotrephes, however, will have to answer for his behaviour: the Elder is no private individual, but one who is capable of speaking authoritatively to Diotrephes and to the church which he dominates. How far he could be sure of asserting his authority successfully cannot be determined, but presumably if Diotrephes could carry the church with him against the Elder their fellowship with the churches which did acknowledge the Elder's authority would be endangered. C. H. Dodd suggests that the preservation of this letter is an argument of some weight in favour of the view that the Elder's appeal was successful.[12] The charges which Diotrephes brought up against the Elder and his associates amounted to sheer nonsense (the verb *phlyareō*, here rendered 'prate', means 'talk nonsense'), but they were malicious nevertheless, and accompanied by malicious actions, for he backed up his own refusal to receive the messengers by forbidding others to welcome them, and excommunicating[13] them if they did. The same verb *epidechomai* is used for 'receive' in verse 10 as in verse 9; RSV varies its rendering

of the word by translating it 'welcome' in this verse.[14] If 3 John
were indeed written to a member of the congregation addressed in
2 John, we should certainly have a piquant situation: the Elder
urges the church not to accept visitors who do not bring 'the
teaching of Christ' with them, but the visitors who are actually
turned away are the Elder's own delegates![15] It is improbable,
however, that the same church is in question; even so, the boycott
was an ecclesiastical weapon which could be used by more than
one party to a dispute.

5   EXHORTATION (verse 11)

**V. 11   Beloved, imitate not that which is evil, but that
which is good. He that doeth good is of God: he that doeth
evil hath not seen God.**

Diotrephes and persons like him are no fit examples for Gaius
or any one else to follow. Happily, there are better examples –
those who do good and not evil, and show thus that they belong
to the family of God (cf. 1 John 3. 10). The contrast between the
two types is summed up in a characteristic Johannine antithesis,
on the same lines as those laid down in 1 John 3. 4–10 (especially
verse 6). It is in Christ that God is seen, and to see Christ is to
become like Him (John 12. 45; 14. 9; 1 John 3. 2).

6   RECOMMENDATION OF DEMETRIUS (verse 12)

**V. 12   Demetrius hath the witness of all *men*, and of the
truth itself: yea, we also bear witness; and thou knowest that
our witness is true.**

If Diotrephes provides an example to be avoided, here is one
whose example can be safely followed. Demetrius is apparently
the bearer of this letter, and the letter incorporates the Elder's
commendation of him. In the circumstances it was useless to give
him a letter commending him to the church in that place, for
Diotrephes would see to it that the letter and its bearer were alike
refused. But John is persuaded that Gaius will live up to his

reputation for hospitality and give Demetrius a welcome. Those
referred to as 'all', from whom Demetrius receives a good report,
may be the generality of Christians in the region where he is known,
but we cannot exclude the probability that, in terms of the quali-
fications for a 'bishop' specified in 1 Tim. 3. 7, he was 'well thought
of by outsiders'. The statement that Demetrius in addition
received a good report from 'the truth itself' may mean that, apart
from any human voice, the facts themselves testified in his favour;
but it is more probable that 'the truth' is here personal, denoting
our Lord (cf. John 14. 6) and that we should translate: 'the Truth
Himself'. Similar language is used by Papias of Hierapolis, a
member of the same school a generation or so later, who tells how
he sought out those who had been in touch with companions and
eyewitnesses of Jesus, so that he might ascertain and record the
commandments 'given to faith by the Lord and proceeding from
the Truth Himself'[16] (the same phrase as here). The Elder adds
his personal testimony, based on first-hand knowledge of Demetrius,
and Gaius knows that the Elder's testimony is trustworthy. The
words 'thou knowest that our witness is true' are remarkably
similar to those appended as a postscript in John 21. 24, presumably
by those associates of the Beloved Disciple who were responsible
for publishing the Fourth Gospel: 'we know that his witness is
true'.[17]

7 PERSONAL NOTES (verses 13-14)

**V. 13 I had many things to write unto thee, but I am
unwilling to write *them* to thee with ink and pen: v. 14 but
I hope shortly to see thee, and we shall speak face to face.**

This note is very similar to that at the end of the previous letter
(2 John 12). The imperfect tense 'I had' may be epistolary, in
which case it should be rendered 'I have'; but this is not necessarily
so. There were no doubt delicate personal and ecclesiastical
questions which could more conveniently be discussed orally than
in a letter. The phrase 'with ink and pen' takes the place of 'with
paper and ink' in 2 John 12; the 'pen' is a reed-pen (Gr. *kalamos*)

'reed'). John's intention to see Gaius 'shortly' or 'immediately' (Gr. *eutheōs*) may best be taken to mean very soon after the arrival of his letter; the letter prepares Gaius for his visit (perhaps he was about to set out on a circuit of the churches in his sphere of interest, including also the church addressed in 2 John). The phrase 'speak face to face' (lit. 'mouth to mouth') is repeated from 2 John 12 and is discussed briefly in the comment on that verse (p. 143).

8 FINAL GREETING (verse 15)

V. 15 Peace *be* **unto thee. The friends salute thee. Salute the friends by name.**

'Peace to you' is a common Hebraic and Semitic greeting (Heb. *shalom 'alekha*; Arab. *salaam 'alaika*). The 'friends' who send their greetings are those with whom the Elder found himself at the time of writing – perhaps the members of the church referred to as 'the children of your elect sister' in 2 John 13, if both letters were written at the same time. Correspondingly, the 'friends' to whom greetings are sent – 'by name', that is individually – are those who were with Gaius at the time, probably members of his church who, despite Diotrephes, were well-disposed towards John and his messengers.[18]

NOTES

1. For the tense 'I rejoiced' or 'I rejoice' (Gr. *echarēn*) cf. 2 John 4 (p. 139). Here AV, RSV and NEB agree with RV text in the use of the past tense.
2. Its omission in Codex Sinaiticus and a few other authorities may be due to the analogy of 2 John 4.
3. *Didache* 12. 1; 13. 1 (see pp. 142 f.).
4. J. A. T. Robinson, 'The Destination and Purpose of the Johannine Epistles', *Twelve NT Studies* (London, 1962), p. 132.
5. So the third corrector of Codex Sinaiticus with several other Greek witnesses and the Latin and Syriac versions. This depicting of the letter in question as one which he would have written but did not actually write may have been intended to get rid of the disturbing thought that an apostolic letter was lost.
6. So a corrector of minuscule 424.
7. So a corrector of minuscule 326, reading *autē tē ekklēsia* for *ti tē ekklēsia*.
8. Cf. R. Eisler, *The Enigma of the Fourth Gospel* (London, 1938), pp. 172 f.; for the view that 1 and 2 John were 'dedicatory' or covering letters com-

mending to the readers' acceptance copies of the Gospel of John, which accompanied them; and that it was this Gospel that Diotrephes refused to accept, excommunicating those who did accept it. Diotrephes is characterized by Eisler as 'the first of the *Alogoi*' – a disparaging designation given to a group of people towards the end of the second century who rejected the Fourth Gospel (disparaging because it could mean not only 'devoid of the *logos*' in the sense of John 1. 1–14 but also 'devoid of *logos*' in the sense of 'reason', like the 'irrational animals' of Jude 10; 2 Pet. 2. 12). Eisler's theories were invariably brilliant, but almost invariably unconvincing.

9. So A. Harnack, *Über den dritten Johannesbrief* = *TU* 15, 3 (Leipzig, 1897), pp. 21 ff., followed by R. Bultmann, *The Johannine Epistles* (Philadelphia, 1973, p. 101), according to whom the conflict was between the new episcopate under which local churches asserted their autonomy and the old province-wide missionary organization which was at this time under the leadership of the Elder.

10. *The Johannine Epistles* (London, 1946), p. 164.

11. As against W. Bauer, *Rechtgläubigkeit und Ketzerei im ältesten Christentum²* (Tübingen, 1963), p. 97, who calls Diotrephes a heresiarch. Conversely, R. Bultmann (*The Johannine Epistles*, p. 101) agrees with E. Käsemann ('Ketzer und Zeuge', *ZTK* 48, 1951, pp. 292 ff.) that Diotrephes represents an inchoate orthodoxy suspicious of the supposed gnostic tendencies of Johannine theology, but dismisses as fantastic his view that Diotrephes actually excommunicated the Elder.

12. *The Johannine Epistles*, p. 165.

13. The same verb (*ekballō*) is used in John 9. 34 f. for what appears to be expulsion from the synagogue.

14. Similarly NEB varies the rendering and translates here: 'he refuses to receive our friends'.

15. Cf. A. Ehrhardt, *The Framework of the New Testament Stories* (Manchester, 1964), pp. 169 f.; he thinks that Diotrephes refused the Elder and his associates because, in his eyes, they did not bring the 'teaching of Christ' and suggests that the judgment 'prating against us with wicked words' would have been phrased 'very differently had there been an authoritative "Apostles' Creed" to pinpoint Diotrephes's heretical views'.

16. Quoted by Eusebius, *Hist. Eccl.* iii. 39. 3. Cf. p. 136.

17. Cf. what is said in reference to the effusion of blood and water from the pierced side of Jesus on the cross: 'he who saw it has borne witness – his witness is true' (John 19. 35).

18. As at the end of the first and second letters, a few later manuscripts add the liturgical 'Amen', but it is absent from the Received Text, and therefore from AV. (In many editions what is here given as verse 15 appears as the continuation of verse 14.)

INDEX